CULTURE SHOCK!

SUCCEED IN BUSINESS

The essential guide for business and investment

Taiwan

Kevin Chambers

Graphic Arts Center Publishing Company
Portland, Oregon

Photo credits:
All photographs courtesy of Kwang Hwa Publishing and
Taipei Economic and Cultural Office, Houston.

This book is published by special
arrangement with Times Editions Pte Ltd
Times Centre, 1 New Industrial Road, Singapore 536196
International Standard Book Number 1-55868-421-2
Library of Congress Catalog Number 98-85901
Graphic Arts Center Publishing Company
P.O. Box 10306 • Portland, Oregon 97210 • (503) 226-2402

Printed in Singapore

Contents

Appendices

This book is dedicated to Mildred, Cathy, and Grey Chambers

Acknowledgements

Peter Osborne and the Australian Business Centre, Paul Brekke and the American Institute in Taiwan, Geraldine Mesenas and Harlinah Whyte of Times Publishing, the Taipei Economic and Cultural Office in Houston, Lynda Silva, Bill and Betty Cote, PHS Consulting, Frank Keating, Ron Rosenfeld, Kwang Hwa Publishing (photographs) and Tung-chiang Yang.

Introduction

The impetus for this book arose from a respect for the Taiwanese business people and what they had achieved over the past four decades. How, I wanted to know, could a country smaller than the American state of Florida develop from an agricultural backwater in the 1950s to a trading and manufacturing powerhouse in the 1990s? What kind of people are these Taiwanese?

This book also arose from a personal dissatisfaction with a genre of international business books that do little more than restate the pamphlets and press releases of self-promoting governments. Why, I thought, can't business books tell it like it is and include unpleasant topics like corruption, politics and red tape? I wrote this book because it is the type of book I wanted when I started looking for information on doing business in Taiwan many years ago. What did I want? I wanted something that offered the essentials of Taiwan's macroeconomic policies and its culture, as well as made frank observations about the day-to-day behaviour of the country's businesses and government.

The reader who picks this book is likely someone with the knowledge that in order to be a player in the global marketplace of the future, his or her business must have the right strategy to succeed in Taiwan. The purpose of this book, then, is to improve that strategy and to make its implementation easier and less costly. As this required a depth and breadth of knowledge and experience beyond my own, I called upon a range of experienced business people for their advice. Many Taiwanese business people and government officials in Taiwan provided their perspectives, as did business people from several countries and professions. Taiwanese, Chinese, Singaporeans, Americans, Mexicans, Australians, Koreans and many others graciously shared their personal experiences of doing business in Taiwan.

Change happens quickly in Taiwan. In the early 1980s, a number of Taiwanese were jailed for supporting the establishment of an opposition party (to the Kuomintang Party). By the mid-1990s, the Republic of China on Taiwan had evolved into an open democracy with a lively multiparty system. Change is no less dramatic on the business front. In the course of a few years, Taiwan progressed from putting LCD clocks in pens to manufacturing leading edge semiconductors. Consequently, this book focuses on presenting information and experiences that will be of value for years to come. Much of the information included is culture-based and should remain relevant as long as Taiwan is Taiwanese.

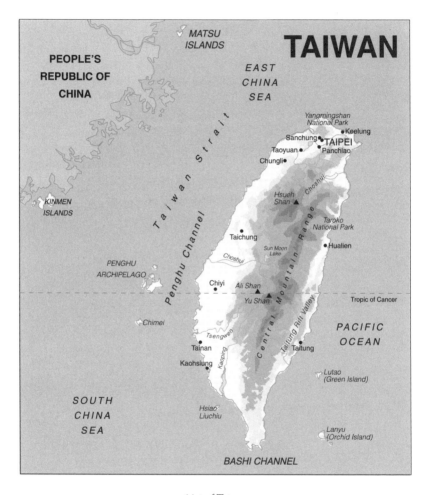

Map of Taiwan

Chapter 1

An Overview of Taiwan

Location and Topography

The tobacco leaf-shaped island of Taiwan lies about 160 kilometres off the south eastern coast of mainland China. Located midway between Japan and Hong Kong, Taiwan sits astride one of the busiest shipping lanes in the world.

The island is just under 400 km long and 145 km wide at its widest point. The southern tip of the island is 350 km north of the Philippines and the northern tip is 1,000 km south-west of Japan. The Tropic of Cancer bisects south-central Taiwan. The Central Mountains run from the north to the south of Taiwan and about two-thirds of the island is covered with forested peaks. Taiwan covers an area of about 36,000 square kilometres and is slightly smaller than the Netherlands.

In addition to the main island, the Taiwan province also includes the Penghu Archipelago—a cluster of 64 islands previously known as the Pescadores.

Climate

Taiwan is sub-tropical with average temperatures of 21.7° Celsius in the north and 24° C in the south. The island is hot and humid and each May, summer arrives with the rainy season. The rains diminish after June, but the miserable heat and humidity run through September, with daytime temperatures ranging from 27° C to 35° C. The mild winters are lamentably short and last only from December to February.

Visiting business people should be prepared for the rain, heat and humidity of Taiwan's summer. On rainy summer days, the heat and humidity can be overwhelming. It is the kind of humidity you can hear. The only way to fight it is to avoid overexertion and to wear clothes that breath well, like materials made of cotton.

During Taiwan's short winters, sweaters may be necessary, especially in air-conditioned restaurants. Whether it is the rainy season or otherwise, always carry an umbrella with you. Climate is what you expect. Weather is what you get.

Taiwan's Business Centres

The largest business centres in Taiwan are Taipei, Kaohsiung, Taichung, Tainan and Keelung. Taipei, the capital, has almost three million residents. Kaohsiung, the second largest city, has a population less than half of Taipei.

Taipei

Taipei is the political, governmental and business centre of Taiwan. The population of almost three million people is expanding rapidly, as more Taiwanese from other cities move into Taipei each year. Most of Taiwan's largest companies have their headquarters in the capital. All foreign embassies and unofficial representative offices are also located in Taipei.

Taipei is clearly the financial capital of Taiwan. The Taiwan Stock Exchange (TAIEX), the Bank of Taiwan, the Import-Export Bank and most of the island's commercial banks are located here. A number of foreign banks and multinational accounting firms have also set up their Taiwan headquarters in Taipei.

The city of Taipei is ringed with factories that deal in chemicals, electronics, machinery and plastics. Although the transportation infrastructure has improved greatly in the 1990s, traffic into and out of the city is bad. The main highway between Taipei and the Chiang Kai-shek International Airport at Taoyuan is always packed with cars and lorries despite the existence of multiple lanes. A long overdue subway system is under construction, but the project has been fraught with delays and mishaps.

Taiwan's capital, Taipei, is full of people, cars and smog—together with most of Taiwan's business activity.

Visiting business people will find that most of their appointments will be in the corridor stretching from the central train station in Taipei's old downtown eastward to the World Trade Centre on Keelung Road. Most of the new development in Taipei has been in the new eastern part of the city surrounding the World Trade Centre. Depending on where most of your appointments are held—in the old downtown or the eastern city—you will want to choose your hotel location carefully. Getting between the two dipodes of Taipei takes time and patience.

Keelung, 30 km north-east of Taipei, is Taiwan's second largest port and an increasingly integrated part of the Taipei metropolitan area. Keelung has a large population and has become a dynamic suburb of Taipei.

Kaohsiung, Taiwan's second largest city, is a major industrial centre located at the south western tip of Taiwan. Kaohsiung is one of the world's top ten general ports.

Kaohsiung

Taiwan's second largest city, Kaohsiung, is the epicentre of southern Taiwan's economy. Situated 300 km south of Taipei, Kaohsiung hugs Taiwan's south-west coast, seeming to distance itself from Taipei as much as possible.

Kaohsiung is an industrial, port city, boasting one of the busiest and most modern harbours in the world.

Business people familiar with Japan often compare Kaohsiung to Japan's second largest city, Osaka. More commercial than Taipei, Kaohsiung's business people dismiss Taipei (as Osakans dismiss Tokyo) as a self-absorbed government enclave that siphons off too much of the nation's resources. Kaohsiung people tend to be direct, entrepreneurial and spirited. They are great business people.

A banquet or business luncheon in Kaohsiung is often a lively affair, more so than in Taipei. The exuberance of Kaohsiung comes through loud and clear. At banquets, people walk from table to table toasting and talking. At the end of the event, many of the attendees challenge one another to down whole pitchers or bowls of wine (with resounding shouts of *"ganbei"* or "cheers" in Mandarin).

Kaohsiung is Taiwan's busiest port and is the third largest container shipping port in the world, after Hong Kong and Singapore. Investments of over $11 billion are under way to create Taiwan's only deep-water harbour in Kaohsiung. The city is home to the island's only international airport outside Taipei.

Kaohsiung is also Taiwan's largest manufacturing centre. One can drive for miles through what seems like endless stretches of industrial complex. China Shipbuilding, China Steel Corporation, China Petroleum and many aluminium, oil, plastics and sugar processing plants dominate Kaohsiung's heavy industrial base.

Taichung

Taichung is the island's third largest city. Known for its colleges and cultural facilities, Taichung has become an economic boom town in recent years. The development of an international port in the western part of the city has accelerated the development of the manufacturing sector in and around Taichung. The city is home to many of Taiwan's largest food, textile, furniture, machinery and leather goods manufacturers. Taiwan's machine tool industry is also concentrated in Taichung.

Centrally located, Taichung (its name literally means "centre of Taiwan" in Mandarin) is blessed with an efficient port and a good diversity of industry and commerce. Taichung's citizens enjoy the highest per capita income in Taiwan. They also enjoy the island's mildest weather.

Tainan

Taiwan's fourth largest city is also its historical and cultural heart. For more than 200 years, Tainan (literally means "south Taiwan") was the capital of Taiwan. Today, Tainan is becoming the centre of Taiwan's information technology industry. In addition, Taiwan's second science-based business park is being built near Tainan.

Only 50 km north of Kaohsiung, the industrial areas of Tainan are beginning to merge with those of Kaohsiung. Textiles, chemicals, electronics and leather goods industries dominate Tainan's industrial sector.

Natural Resources

Taiwan has limited mineral resources. The island has minor deposits of coal, natural gas and petroleum. However, Taiwan does have a significant supply of marble, which has been estimated at close to 350 million tonnes.

Taiwan depends heavily upon imported energy to fuel its economy. Over 90% of Taiwan's commercial energy comes from imported sources, primarily crude oil.

Taiwan has considerably more agricultural resources than mineral resources. The island produces the following crops:

- Sugar cane
- Vegetables
- Rice
- Citrus fruits
- Pineapples

The People

Except for the approximately 350,000 aborigines, the people of Taiwan originate from the Chinese mainland, mainly from the coastal province of Fukien (also called Fujian).

The official language used in Taiwan is Mandarin Chinese. However, in the countryside, Taiwanese—Hoklo, Minnan or southern Fujian dialect—is more frequently used. Hakka (in Chinese, *hakka* means "guest") is also used by some Taiwanese whose ancestors came from Mei (meaning "plum") County in

Canton. Their origin can be traced back to Henan Province in northern China.

Religion

Most Taiwanese, about five million in all, identify themselves as Buddhist and almost one million say they are Taoist. The rest are Protestant (430,000), Roman Catholic (300,000) and Muslim (50,000). Surveys inevitably show that many Taiwanese are followers of more than one faith at a time. The nonexclusive nature of Buddhism and Taoism leave room for multiple allegiances. For example, it is not uncommon to see people who claim to be Buddhist worshipping at a Taoist temple.

The Chinese religious belief systems provide a guardian deity for almost every aspect of life. Chinese deities revered in Taiwan, notably Kuan Yin, the goddess of mercy, and Matsu, the goddess of the sea, all had their origins in the Chinese mainland. Taoism and other indigenous Chinese religions, as well as imported religions like Buddhism, Christianity and Islam, also came to Taiwan via the mainland.

Population Trends

Taiwan is the second most densely populated country in the world (Bangladesh is the densest) with an average of 598 persons per sq. km as of 1997. According to the 1990 census, Taiwan's population had exceeded the 20 million mark. By 1998, the population was estimated to be approximately 21.8 million. The population growth rate is 0.9%.

About 9.4 million Taiwanese are employed in the workforce. Of these, approximately 47% are in the service sector, 40% are in the industrial sector and 12% are in the agricultural or fishing sectors. Taiwan has a labour participation rate of 57%.

More Taiwanese Are Seeing the World

As Taiwanese become more affluent, more and more of them travel the world. Departures from Taiwan are rising at about 9% every year. In 1997, there were 6,161,900 outbound departures from Taiwan. Asian cities remain the primary leisure destination for the Taiwanese, occupying 78% of the market. Travel analysts predict that outbound tourism from Taiwan will continue to grow steadily and that Taiwan will hold its place as Asia's chief generator of tourists, after Japan.

Education

Schools in Taiwan continue to stress rote learning and obedience to authority over creative thinking and reasoning skills. Curriculums are rigid and sluggish to change.

Until recently, this system produced disciplined but politically docile workers. Much of the docility has gone out of the workforce in recent years. The working population's interest in politics has increased with growth in per capita income. Some economists, both within Taiwan and abroad, are beginning to question whether the Taiwanese workforce is prepared to rise to the next level of

Learning the Chinese Way
In the early 1980s, I had the opportunity to teach graduate-level business students at one of Taiwan's most respected private universities. I was struck by both the respect the students showed their teachers and their unquestioning nature. I had great difficulty getting the students to ask questions or voice opinions. When I had occasion to watch how Chinese professors taught their classes, I finally understood why my students were so "docile". Most of my Chinese counterparts stood in front of the class and read from their books the entire class period while their students took notes. I compared this with my own American university education where the culture was such that students did not hesitate to question what the professor told them.

> **My Daughter Speaks English!**
> I once walked into a back alley curio shop in Hualien on Taiwan's remote eastern coast. The excited shop owner made me wait until his daughter could be summoned to take my payment for a small granite chess piece. Although a conversation was not necessary to make the purchase, she explained in halting English that her family had spent a lot to send her to an English school and they wanted to make certain they got their money's worth.

productivity and innovation. Some fear that unless the country invests more into basic technology research and new educational techniques, the country's growth rate cannot be sustained.

The private sector has a long tradition of supplementing and even replacing insufficient government education. This is especially true in the area of English language instruction. *Buxibans,* or cram schools, offer English language classes to students who need improvement, primarily to enable them to pass entrance examinations for the best high schools and universities. Buxibans are expensive and usually employ foreign teachers whose native language is English. Most of the teachers are young American, British or Australian graduates.

In Taiwan, English is not just a tool for international communication but also a symbol of prestige. Children who can speak English and perhaps even go off to college in the United States and other countries are a source of pride to their parents. While many of the students who study English might never use it, there is still the great "What if?" factor that is important to their parents, employers and ultimately themselves. What if they have a chance to travel abroad or to make an important sale to a foreigner?

Infrastructure
For years, Taiwan's infrastructure development lagged far behind its reputation as an economic powerhouse. In the 1990s, the

authorities have made significant progress on its infrastructure development programme. These efforts, however, have not kept pace with demands.

New airports and highways are being built, ports have been upgraded and a new highspeed railway is in the works. However, Taiwan remains behind the curve on power generation capacity. Other basic needs, such as passable highways, are still lacking.

Transportation
Taiwanese drive across their tiny country as if someone is chasing them. The best way to deal with this is to let someone else do the driving for you.

Buses
City buses are frequent and plentiful, but a true challenge for non-Chinese speakers. Destination signs on the buses and at bus stops are in Chinese only. If you want to learn the system, an English route book is available at station kiosks. Fares differ according to the route and distance travelled. A single section fare in Taipei is NT$12 for air-conditioned buses. Pay upon boarding or alighting. Ticket booklets can be purchased at station kiosks or sidewalk newsstands.

Highway bus services connect Taipei to all the major cities and scenic spots. The government-owned Taiwan Motor Transport and private United Highway Bus Corporation both provide intercity, air-conditioned express buses. Fares are reasonable. For information and reservations in Taipei, you can call the various bus terminals.

Car Rentals
Only Bangkok taxi drivers would feel comfortable driving in Taiwan's major cities. I do not recommend driving in Taiwan because of the heavy traffic and limited parking spaces. It is easier to drive in rural areas. To rent a car, credit cards or sizeable deposits

Cars, buses, taxis and motorcycles crowd Taiwan's cities and make getting about a challenge.
Subways and light rail projects are underway to alleviate the congestion.

are required in addition to an international or Taiwan driver's licence. A good alternative is chauffeur-driven cars available from your hotel.

Most people in Taiwan drive on the right-hand side of the road. Illegal parking can result in a fine of NT$1,500, with the possibility of your car being relocated elsewhere—good luck finding it.

Taxis

Taxis are the best way to get around the cities for appointments. Except during rainstorms when the demand outpaces supply, taxis are easy to flag down. If you are having difficulty getting a taxi to stop for you during rush hour or in a storm, just hold up two fingers to indicate you are willing to pay twice the metered rate. Three fingers if you are really desperate.

Very few taxi drivers speak English, so have your destination written down in Chinese to indicate where you are heading before starting out. Carry a hotel card to show the driver when you want to return to your hotel.

Taxi meters start at NT$65 for the first 1.8 km and NT$5 for each additional 350 metres. Waiting time is NT$5 for every three minutes. Between 11 p.m. and 6 a.m., surcharges apply. Receipts are available upon request.

Taxi drivers do not generally expect a tip, but you can leave any small change left from the fee.

Trains

The Taiwan Railway Administration provides fully electrified round-the-island services from Taipei to the main cities both on the western and eastern coasts. The trains are frequent, comfortable, efficient and inexpensive. Express trains, depending on comfort and speed, are divided into three classes with slightly differing prices. Sleep service is also available on night trains between Taipei and Kaohsiung, and the travel time is five to six hours.

Trains are packed with travellers on weekends and holidays. Train travel in Taiwan is convenient and inexpensive. It takes only five hours to get from Taipei to Kaohsiung by train.

Taiwan's Rapid Transit System

Classes of Trains	Conditions
Tzuchiang*	Air-conditioned express trains
Chukuang*	Air-conditioned and a little slower than the Tzuchiang
Fuhsing*	Air-conditioned. Slower than Chukuang and not as comfortable
Pingkuai	No air-conditioning and no reserved seats. Many stops but cheap
Putung	Really slow. Really hot and uncomfortable but really cheap

* express trains

Seat reservations for express trains are necessary. Reservations can be made at the main railway station up to seven days before you plan to travel. A return ticket can be bought in advance but the time for the return trip can only be confirmed at the destination point. The business centre or concierge at your hotel should be able to handle this for you.

If you have business in Taipei and Taichung or Kaohsiung, try the comfortable express trains between the cities at least once. It is much faster to fly between Taipei and Kaohsiung, but if time permits, take a daytime trip across the island. The experience is worth it.

On Foot

The crowded sidewalks, heavy traffic and humidity of Taiwan's cities do not make for pleasant walks. Just crossing the streets in some areas can be a challenge. Some of Taipei's and Kaohsiung's large intersections can be confusing, with cars seemingly coming from all directions. On streets such as Taipei's Chungshan North Road, pedestrians are forced to cross the many intersections via subways beneath the streets. A few blocks of this up-and-down walking in humid weather can be exhausting.

Motorbike owners park their machines on the sidewalks and in some areas such as downtown Taipei, the sidewalks can be so packed with illegally parked motorbikes that pedestrians are forced to walk on the roads. Sidewalks in many areas are dangerously uneven and cracked.

In Taipei, a good walk that helps me wind down after a busy day of business meetings is a night-time stroll around the expansive grounds of the Chiang Kai-shek Memorial near downtown. Here, you can see entire families out walking together and groups of good-natured teenagers talking.

You can take good country walks in the mountains surrounding Taipei or in the rural areas of Taiwan. The Tienmu and Yangmingshan National Park areas near Taipei have good footpaths for pleasant walks. It gets very hot and humid from June to August, so it is advisable to walk in the cooler morning or evening hours during this period.

The Economy

The best measure of the economic progress of Taiwan is the per capita income of its citizenry. In 1950, one year after Chiang Kai-shek moved his government and military to Taiwan, per capita income was US$145 a year. Forty-five years later, the official per capita income was almost US$12,500 per year. The *unofficial* per capita income is estimated to be about US$20,000 per year. Why is an unofficial measurement so important? This is because much of Taiwan's economy is undocumented and underground—more on that later. Suffice it to say that Taiwan's economy has boomed in the last half-century and serves as a model of development for other Newly Industrialised Countries (NICs) and NIC wannabes.

After the presidential election of 1996 and the concurrent missile tests by the People's Republic of China (PRC), there was a dramatic shift in sentiment in Taiwan. For the first time in years, the political powers seemed to come to a consensus that much-needed economic reform was achievable. The focus was off politics and back on to achieving economic progress. The two main political parties, the Kuomintang (Nationalist) Party and the New Democratic Party, began working together on pragmatic reforms for the good of the country.

Taiwan has proven to be somewhat immune to the financial crisis that has rocked much of East and Southeast Asia since 1997. Possibly, the island has been sheltered from some of the ups and downs of the region's markets because of Taiwan's protected financial markets and strong central bank.

Taiwan is also not as reliant on foreign capital and technology as some of its neighbours. Tremendous amounts of investments have been flowing into Taiwan's information technology and electronics sectors and almost all of them are generated

Taiwan: A Statistical Overview (1997)

Population	21.7 million
Annual growth rate	0.95%
Workforce	9.4 million
Languages	Mandarin Chinese (official), Taiwanese, Hakka

Education

Years compulsory	nine
Attendance	99.9%
Literacy	94%

Health

Infant mortality rate	0.7%
Life expectancy	71.9 yrs (male); 77.9 yrs (female)

Economy

GDP	US$283.6 billion
Annual growth rate	5.7%
Per capita GNP	US$13,233
Inflation (1996)	3.1%
Fiscal year	Starts 1 July
Natural resources	Small deposits of coal, natural gas, limestone, marble, and asbestos
Agriculture (3.6% of GDP)	Major products: pork, rice, betel nut, sugarcane, poultry, shrimp and eel.
Industry (37.4% of GDP)	Major sectors: plastics, textiles, machinery, basic metals, transport items, chemicals and petrochemicals, and electronics and computer products

domestically. The Taiwanese tend to invest profits back into their industries to upgrade productivity at home. At the same time, foreign investors continue to pour investment dollars into Taiwan in the belief that the island's business environment is both safe and full of potential. Most Taiwanese companies are small to medium-sized operations run by well-educated owner-managers who can move quickly to take advantage of fleeting opportunities.

In addition, Taiwan is moving quickly to privatise many of its large, state-owned enterprises and banks. The country's energy and telecommunications enterprises are being privatised, as are the largest state-run banks. The government's objective is to improve competitiveness through privatisation. The government is expected to earn about US\$5 billion per year through this privatisation movement.

International Economic Relations

Taiwan's economy cannot exist in a vacuum. So much of Taiwan's economic health depends on its economic relations with other countries such that fluctuations in the economies of Taiwan's major export markets have a consequential impact on the island. If Japan, Hong Kong, Southeast Asia or the United States suffer an economic downturn, the ripple effect soon reaches Taiwan. For example, if Southeast Asian importers cannot afford to import Taiwanese goods, Taiwan's exports fall dramatically.

Taiwan has worked diligently to maintain economic relations with other countries even as most of its major trading partners have downgraded political ties with the Republic of China (ROC) in Taiwan. Even as Japan, the United States and the European nations have de-recognised the ROC government in Taipei and opted in favour of diplomatic recognition of the PRC government in Beijing, Taipei has kept economic and cultural relations with these nations open. In most cases, economic and cultural relations have been handled by "unofficial" organisations set up to provide functions normally performed by embassies and consulates. These

29

functions include visa issuance, bilateral relations, trade development and cultural exchanges.

For example, after the United States de-recognised Taipei in 1979, Taiwan replaced its embassy and consulates in the United States with an organisation called the Taipei Economic and Cultural Office (TECO)*. In turn, the United States replaced its embassy in Taipei with an organisation called the American Institute in Taiwan (AIT). Both the TECO and AIT issue visas, engage in trade development work, gather economic intelligence, promote cultural exchanges and a myriad of other duties that are normally performed by embassies. In fact, both organisations are staffed by employees of the respective country's ministries of foreign affairs and commerce who temporarily "resign" from their government positions during their postings in the other country. In effect, it is all an elaborate diplomatic game played to appease the People's Republic of China, which insists that other countries have no diplomatic ties with Taipei.

The same charade is carried on between Taiwan and many other countries with which the ROC government has no diplomatic ties. The names of the associations or "unofficial embassies" differ from country to country, but the game remains the same. In Japan, Taiwan's unofficial embassy is called the Taipei Economic and Cultural Representative Office. In Singapore, it is called the Taipei Representative Office and in France, it is the Centre Asiatique de Promotion Economique et Commercial. In addition, much of Taiwan's commercial relations are carried out in other countries by a ROC government organisation called the Far East Trade Services, Inc. (FETS).

From 1950 to 1990, Taiwan kept its own market largely closed to foreign imports and competition, and strove hard to export to other markets. While Taiwan dropped most of its protectionist

---

* This organisation was originally known as the Coordination Council for North American Affairs (CCNAA) but was changed to TECO in 1996.

regulations in the mid-1990s, the government still clings to a policy of protecting its agricultural sector and some sections of the manufacturing industry. To further protect its home-grown industries it considers to be strategic, Taiwan also maintains a long list of items banned from importation and continues to prohibit foreign investment in many of these industries. Although these barriers are an obstacle to Taiwan's closer integration with the other countries of North and East Asia, the ROC government considers the protection of these industries a national security issue and, therefore, of paramount importance.

Taipei has expressed some concern over the possibility of Japan's economic domination of Taiwan. The country has long suffered large trade imbalances with Japan and the authorities have taken steps to promote more trade with the United States, Southeast Asia and Europe in an effort to lessen its dependence on Japanese products.

Taiwan's Economic Strategy
Taiwan will likely continue to pursue trade and investment liberalisation as a key strategy to fuel development. Falling levels of foreign investment in Taiwan has prompted Taipei to improve its investment incentives and climate. Some restrictions have been dropped and the application procedures for both inbound and outbound investments have been simplified and shortened.

Taiwan Bets On Regional Business Hub Strategy
The ROC government has embarked on a strategy to develop Taiwan into what they have dubbed the Asia-Pacific Regional Operations Centre (APROC), a regional business hub for multinational corporations. The APROC concept has been marketed heavily by Taiwan since it was launched in 1995. Taiwan, already home to the regional headquarters of a number of high-tech multinationals, could, so the authorities thought, parley this into becoming the regional communications and business hub.

The sales pitch has been successful to a certain extent, but the hub strategy has a significant weakness—the disconnection between Taiwan and the largest market in the region, the People's Republic of China. For national security reasons, the ROC government maintains a ban on most direct trade, communications and transport between Taiwan and the PRC. While two sea routes (from Kaohsiung to the PRC ports of Fuzhou and Xiamen) were opened between Taiwan and the PRC in 1997, multinational companies still cannot effectively cover the PRC market from a business centre in Taiwan unless the transactions are done from another location outside of Taiwan.

As long as cross-straits air connections are forbidden, it will be infeasible for most multinational companies to utilise Taiwan as a regional hub for distribution. Having to re-route shipments through third country (or Hong Kong) airports adds substantial costs to the distribution formula of getting goods from Taiwan to cities in the PRC.

Taiwan's strengths—a well-educated and hardworking populace, democratic institutions and a sound business climate—still make it a strong contender for regional "hubdom", at least for some companies, However, high cost of doing business, traffic congestion, restrictions on expatriates and foreign businesses, and lack of direct trade with the People's Republic of China lessen the likelihood that Taiwan will become the regional hub for multinationals that the authorities want it to be.

Upgrading Taiwan's High-Tech Industries

The government's key economic goal is to upgrade the country's value-added industries. The technological development of the country's information technology and aerospace industries are top of the list. Taiwan's leaders realise that rising production costs have resulted in the moving of Taiwan's labour-intensive industries such as textiles, clothing and toy manufacturing—the foundation of the country's industrial takeoff—to mainland China, Vietnam and

The Taipei Aerospace Technology Exhibition at the Taipei World Trade Centre showcases Taiwan's advances in developing an indigenous aerospace industry for both self defence and export purposes.

Indonesia. Taiwan has, as a result, invested huge amounts of resources into developing its high-tech industries and infrastructure to attract more domestic and foreign investment into its information technology and aerospace sectors.

The government has focused on stimulating investments in high-tech industries by developing science-based parks such as Hsinchu near Taipei. The government has also designed tax breaks and other subsidies for selected industries.

Concern Over Economic Ties with the PRC

The ROC government is concerned about the growing interdependence between Taiwan and mainland China. While the authorities in Taipei have maintained the ban on most direct trade and communications between Taiwan and the People's Republic of China, Taiwan's businesses have been investing heavily in the coastal areas of the PRC and trade dependence on the mainland has been rising.

Approximately 10%–20% of Taiwan's total trade is with China. Taiwan's exports to mainland China and Hong Kong reached US$29.3 billion in 1997 (a 7% increase from the previous year), even though China's total imports grew by only 2.5%. Exports to mainland China and Hong Kong have accounted for 38% of Taiwan's export increase since 1990. This has been a major source of Taiwan's GDP growth. Most of Taiwan's exports to China appear to be in the form of Taiwanese factory investments in China. Imports from the Chinese mainland have also been growing in recent years. The major items imported include Chinese herbal medicines, footwear, polyester fibre, cotton, furs and feathers.

While Taiwan's authorities are concerned about the increasing economic dependence on the mainland, they also seek to avoid the regional isolation that could shut Taiwan out of future Asian trading blocks. This fear of isolation has driven the ROC government to seek limited ties with the mainland.

Representatives from Taiwan and the PRC met in Singapore in 1993 for the first of a series of talks on political and economic issues. The same concern has also prompted Taiwan to become a member of the Asia Pacific Economic Council (APEC), together with China and Hong Kong, under the name "Chinese Taipei".

Taiwan's Foreign Trade

Without trade, Taiwan would be little more than an obstruction in the sea lanes between Japan and Singapore. This is, however, not the case. Following an export-driven strategy, the entrepreneurs of Taiwan have put their country on the map.

Since the 1960s, exports have fuelled Taiwan's growth. In the 1980s and early 1990s, Taiwan ran huge trade surpluses that inflated the island's foreign exchange reserves to as much as US$100.41 billion in June 1995. Since 1995, Taiwan's foreign exchange reserves have hovered around US$85 billion.

Taiwan's Foreign Trade Statistics, 1986–1996
(US$ million)

Year	Exports	Imports	Total Trade	Balance
1996	115,982.20	101,278.10	217,260.30	14,704.10
1995	111,688.10	103,571.60	215,259.70	8,116.50
1994	93,056.30	85,359.20	178,415.50	7,697.10
1993	84,910.00	77,000.00	161,910.00	7,910.00
1992	81,470.30	71,976.60	153,446.90	9,493.70
1991	76,178.30	62,860.60	139,038.90	13,317.70
1990	67,214.50	54,716.00	121,930.50	12,498.50
1989	66,304.00	52,265.30	118,569.30	14,038.70
1988	60,667.40	49,672.80	110,340.20	10,994.60
1987	53,678.80	34,983.40	88,662.20	18,695.40
1986	39,861.50	24,181.50	64,043.00	15,680.00

(Last updated: 9/2/1997)

In 1991, under pressure from the United States and in anticipation of joining the World Trade Organisation or WTO (known as GATT at the time), Taiwan started an import promotion programme to open up its economy by reducing import tariffs and encouraging the importation of foreign products. Within a year, Taiwan's trade surplus had fallen to US$9.5 billion, down nearly 30% from the previous year.

Taiwan's Exports
Over 60% of Taiwan's exports go to just three markets. Most of it (23% each) is absorbed by the United States and Hong Kong (includes trade with the PRC). Japan takes 12% of the exports.

As Taiwan's income level rose, demand for imported, high-quality consumer goods also increased. In recent years, Taiwan has successfully diversified its trade markets, cutting its share of exports to the United States from 49% in 1984 to 23% in 1996. In

---

Taiwan's Leading Export Markets (1996)

Country	Percentage of Total Exports
United States	23.2
Hong Kong	23.1
Japan	11.8
Singapore	3.9
Netherlands	3.3

1997, Taiwan's total trade surplus with the United States was US$12.2 billion, a significant amount, no doubt, but a decline from a high of US$17 billion in 1987. Taiwan's dependence on the US market will continue to decrease, as its exports to Southeast Asia and the PRC grow, and its efforts to develop European markets produce results.

Trade with the People's Republic of China is expected to grow and be focused on Hong Kong. Taiwan will continue to experience multi-billion dollar trade surpluses with Hong Kong. Since the New Taiwan dollar's exchange rate is tied to that of the US dollar, Taiwan's trade with Japan will continue to fluctuate with the relative appreciation or depreciation of the Japanese yen versus the US dollar. When the yen appreciates against the US dollar as it did in 1994, Taiwan's exports to Japan will rise as they become cheaper to Japanese buyers.

For years, the authorities in Taiwan have tried to reduce their huge trade deficit with Japan. While they have succeeded in increasing Taiwan's exports to Japan, this increase is growing much slower than the rate of imports from Japan.

Taiwan is turning increasingly to Southeast Asia as part of its diversification of exports plan. In 1986, only 5% of ROC exports went to this region. Eight years later, in 1994, the figure had jumped to 11.5% (US$11.5 billion).

Taiwan's Major Export Items

Taiwan's six major export items in 1997, consisting of more than 60% of total exports, were mechanical appliances, electrical machinery, plastics and plastics-related products, transportation equipment, synthetic fabrics and steel products. The two major export categories—mechanical appliances and electrical machinery—accounted for almost half of Taiwan's exports.

The computer industry has become the single major export industry in Taiwan and accounts for most of the items that make up the two top export categories. The largest category, mechanical appliances, is made up of products such as data processing machine parts, terminals and digital auto data processing machines. The electrical machinery category includes items such as semiconductor chips, computer monitors and silicon wafers. Computer-related exports such as those mentioned above grew at an astounding annual average of 21% over the 1995–1997 period.

Taiwan's Top Exports (1997)

Product Category	Amount (US$ billions)	Percentage of Exports
Total exports	122.08	100
Mechanical appliances	31.84	26.1
Electrical machinery	27.15	22.2
Plastics and articles	6.64	5.4
Transportation equipment	4.81	3.9
Man-made filaments	3.73	3.1
Articles of iron or steel	3.72	3.0
Apparel	3.02	2.5
Iron or steel	2.93	2.4
Toys and sports equipment	2.38	2.0
Textile for industrial use	2.34	1.9

Source: ROC Board of Foreign Trade

In contrast, exports of comparatively lower value-added and labour-intensive products continued to drop. In 1997, toys and sports equipment exports dropped by almost 11% over 1996 totals. Today, toys and sports equipment account for only 2% of Taiwan's exports. Taiwanese companies still make much of the world's toys, but they manufacture and export from their factories in mainland China where labour costs are much lower than in Taiwan.

Imports

Japan and the United States account for over 45% of Taiwan's imports. In 1997, the aggregate value of Taiwan's imports was US$114.4 billion, an increase of 11.8% over the previous year. This was attributable to an increase in domestic demand and investment. Large investments in Taiwan's semiconductor industry resulted in significant increases in the importation of semiconductors and mechanical appliances.

Taiwan's Top Imports (1997)

Product Category	Amount (US$ billions)	Percentage of Imports
Total imports	114.42	100
Electrical machinery	24.96	21.8
Mechanical appliances	16.16	14.1
Mineral fuels	9.09	7.9
Optical instruments	6.03	5.3
Organic chemicals	5.54	4.8
Special products	5.51	4.8
Iron and steel	5.45	4.8
Transportation equipment	3.35	2.9
Plastics and articles	3.08	2.7
Copper and articles	2.13	1.9

Source: ROC Board of Foreign Trade

Japan was the source of 27% of Taiwan's 1996 imports. Major import items from Japan included machinery, electrical, electronic, chemical and metal products, as well as auto parts. Unabated growth (over 10% annually) in Japanese imports has led to a serious trade deficit with Japan, which has tripled from US$3.18 billion to US$14.56 billion in less than 15 years.

The second largest source of Taiwan's imports was the United States. US products comprised 20% of Taiwan's imports in 1996. Imports from Europe and Southeast Asia recorded double digit growth, rising by 17.6% and 24.4% respectively. Agricultural and industrial raw materials accounted for 70.6% of imports, while capital equipment and consumer products made up 16% and 13.4% respectively.

The Political Scene

At the end of World War II, the government of the Republic of China resumed sovereignty over Taiwan. Chinese sovereignty returned to the island after 50 years of Japanese colonial rule. In 1949, the Chinese civil war culminated in a communist victory on the mainland and the Republic of China, or Kuomintang (KMT), government retreated to Taiwan where it has ruled since. Generalissimo Chiang Kai-shek led the ROC government and Kuomintang Party until his death in 1975 at the age of 88. His son, Chiang Ching-kuo, then assumed the presidency.

Chiang Ching-kuo initiated democratic reforms during the last years of his presidency. In 1990, Chiang Ching-kuo's protege, Lee Teng-hui, became the first Taiwan-born president of the Republic of China.

Lee Teng-hui succeeded Chiang Ching-kuo as president when Chiang died on 13 January 1988. In 1990, Lee was elected by the National Assembly to a six-year term, marking the final time a president was elected by the National Assembly. Beginning in 1996, the president and vice president were directly elected to four-year terms by Taiwan's voters. In 1996, Lee Teng-hui was

Political Establishment in Brief

Type
Multi-party democracy. With the direct presidential election in 1996, Taiwan completed its transition from a one-party, authoritarian state to an open, vigorous democracy with three major parties and more than 70 registered parties.

Constitution
25 December 1947

Branches
Five *yuan*: Executive, Legislative (parliament), Judicial, Control, Examination.
Separate National Assembly has certain powers regarding appointment, impeachment and constitutional amendment but has no general legislative functions.

Administrative Subdivisions
Taiwan Province, Fujian Province (for Kinmen and Matsu Islands), Taipei and Kaohsiung Special Municipalities.

Major Political Parties
Chinese Nationalist Party (Kuomintang or KMT); Democratic Progressive Party (DPP); Chinese New Party (CNP).

Suffrage
Universal; over 20 years of age.

elected president in the first presidential election in Taiwan (or in all of China) in which the citizens voted for the candidates directly, rather than through representatives.

This change in the political process is the result of the liberalizing trend that began in the late 1980s when President Chiang Ching-kuo lifted the emergency decree that had been in place since 1948. This decree had granted virtually unlimited powers to the president for use in the anti-communist campaign and provided the basis for nearly four decades of martial law. Until martial law was lifted in 1987, individuals and groups expressing dissenting views were treated harshly.

Since the end of martial law, human rights has dramatically improved in Taiwan and the country has worked to create a democratic political system. Restrictions on the press have greatly diminished, restrictions on personal freedom have been relaxed and the prohibition against the formation of political parties has been lifted.

Taiwan's political system has been dominated by the KMT and until 1986, the party's chairman was also Taiwan's president. Many top political officials are members of the party's Central Standing Committee, which is the chief policy-making organ within the party. As the ruling party, the KMT has filled appointed governmental positions with its members and maintained control over the island.

Since 1986, emerging political parties have challenged the KMT's dominance. Before then, candidates opposing the KMT ran as independents or "nonpartisans" in the elections. Many "nonpartisans" grouped together illegally to create Taiwan's first new political party in over four decades—the Democratic Progressive Party (DPP). Despite the official ban on the formation of political parties, Taiwan authorities did not prohibit the DPP from operating. In 1989, the DPP and other new political parties were legalised and the DPP's influence increased.

The DPP's voice has been an important factor in legislative decisions since 1992 and the DPP's image was significantly enhanced when it won the Taipei mayoral election in December 1994. Its platform includes outspoken positions on some of the most sensitive issues in Taiwanese politics. The DPP maintains that Taiwan is an entity separate from mainland China. This is in contrast to the KMT position that Taiwan and the mainland are both part of "one China". A number of DPP officials, in sharp contrast to the tenets of both KMT and PRC policy, openly advocate independence for Taiwan.

The second major opposition party, the Chinese New Party (CNP), was established in 1993 and has a conservative platform. The CNP emphasises "clean government" and the original KMT focus on reunification with the mainland. Although CNP membership remains small, its influence is considerable, especially in its ability to draw support away from the KMT.

Abolishing the Provincial Government

When the Nationalists retreated to Taiwan and moved the capital of the Republic of China government to the island, they created an anomaly. The island of Taiwan was a province (or state) of the Republic of China, but its borders now coincided with the shrunken borders of the nation. National government agencies and provincial government agencies shared exactly the same territory. The ROC Ministry of Transportation, for example, was responsible for the same geographic region as the Taiwan Provincial Ministry of Transportation. The confusion over which agencies were responsible each region created a good deal of duplication of services.

The confusion created by the overlapping situation was tolerated because the ROC government fully expected to return to the mainland when the communist regime collapsed or was defeated. By the early 1990s, it became apparent to even the most stalwart defenders of the KMT (Kuomintang) that retaking the mainland was not going to happen in the short term. Progressive leaders began thinking of what to do about the jurisdictional duplication of the national and provincial governments.

In 1996, the national government began to slowly dismantle Taiwan's provincial government. The Taiwan provincial government (TPG) consists of 29 principal agencies (ranging from the department of Aboriginal affairs to the department of water resources), with 173 auxiliary agencies and 327,371 TPG employees (80% of whom have a college degree or higher). However, as of September 1998, none of the provincial agencies have been eliminated. No date has been set for this transition.

Other reforms included the central government's takeover and privatisation of the provincial government's three largest commercial banks, Hua Nan Bank, First Bank and Chang Hwa Bank.

Reforms Driven By WTO Membership Desires

A good deal of the reform mood in Taiwan is attributable to the government's desire to join the World Trade Organisation (WTO), the successor organisation to the General Agreement on Tariffs and Trade (GATT).

While the negotiations and preparations for Taiwan's entry into the WTO were nearing completion by 1997, there was general consensus that this could not happen until the PRC was admitted by the WTO. The PRC, like a jealous sibling, has insisted that Taiwan not be admitted to the WTO before the PRC. Never one to refrain from throwing its considerable weight around, the PRC succeeded in intimidating the world community into delaying Taiwan's entry into the WTO. Because the PRC's market reforms fall far short of WTO requirements for admittance (unless special exemptions are allowed), it appears that Taiwan's entry may be considerably delayed.

Is Taiwan Part of a "Greater China" Market?

In international business circles and the academia, the terms "Greater China" and "South China Economic Zone" are bandied about. The business person concerned with Taiwan should not be overly concerned with the concept, however, and should not make the mistake of thinking that Taiwan and the PRC are one market.

What is called Greater China consists of China, Taiwan, Hong Kong and Singapore. Companies in Taiwan, Hong Kong and Singapore have invested so much in the southern provinces of China that the connections there have given rise to the idea of a

South China Economic Zone. So far, the capital flows have been mostly one way—into China. In recent years, however, mainland enterprises have invested heavily in Hong Kong.

The wave of investment in China has begun to change from one focused on production for export to one focused on production for the booming domestic China market. Hong Kong entrepreneurs have led the charge deeper and deeper into China. Hong Kong accounts for about 60% of total foreign investment in China. However, Taiwan is rapidly catching up. Conservative estimates place the annual Taiwanese investment in the mainland at US$1 billion. Since much of the Taiwanese investment goes unreported, it is safe to say that the actual investment level may be much higher.

Chapter 2

Taiwan's History for the Business Person

The Art of War

Why should you care about Taiwan's history? What does history have to do with business today? The reason you should care enough to at least get an overview of Taiwan's history is summed up by Sun Tzu, a Chinese general from the fourth century B.C., in his treatise, "The Art of War":

"Know your enemy, know yourself and your victory will not be threatened. Know the terrain, know the weather and your victory will be complete."

"The reason why the enlightened ruler and the wise general are able to conquer the enemy whenever they lead the army and can achieve victories that surpass those of others is because of foreknowledge."

While Sun Tzu did not have business in mind when he wrote the military classic, *The Art of War*, the principles he promoted are remarkably pertinent in today's competitive business environment. Fortunately, Taiwan is at war only in the sense that its enterprises are world-class competitors battling for a finite number of markets. Any international company that finds itself competing with Taiwanese entrepreneurs and corporations will certainly feel as if it is on the battlefield facing a formidable opponent. It behoves you to know as much about that opponent as you can.

Knowledge of Taiwan's history may be useful to you only from the standpoint that you have an opportunity to subtly let your Taiwanese counterpart know that you have some knowledge of his or her culture and, therefore, of him or her. He or she can take this as a compliment—that you have invested the time to get to know his or her culture—or as a threat—that you are not the kind of person that enters a situation without the knowledge and resources to defend your position. Either way, you win.

An awareness of Taiwan's history and of Chinese culture will also have the added benefit of reducing your chances of committing social blunders. It is challenging enough for foreign visitors to avoid conversational errors related to the side of the political fence their listeners adhere to—pro-reunification versus pro-independence versus status quo. If the visitor is unaware even of the existence of this division, the chances of committing grievous mistakes are compounded.

Among the best ways to prepare for a visit is to read a good book about Taiwan or China. You can find a list of suitable books in the appendix of this book. Most executives lead busy lives, so if not before, at least read these books on the flight to Taiwan. The information will be fresh in your mind upon arrival.

Most business people and dignitaries who visit Taiwan are taken by their hospitable hosts to visit the astonishing National Palace Museum in Taipei's outskirts. Most of China's history is located, quite literally, in the museum's special humidity-controlled rooms. Unfortunately, the visit to the National Palace Museum invariably takes place at the end of the visitor's sojourn in Taiwan after the business is done. See it before you have your first meeting so you can benefit from the insight into Chinese and Taiwanese culture. Besides, it is better, while in a jet-lag, to see the museum rather than try to negotiate a deal in such a condition.

The key to understanding Taiwan's history is to first understand that there is more than one historical perspective. There is a Taiwan history from the viewpoint of the Chinese mainlanders and then there is a Taiwan history from the viewpoint of the Taiwanese. From the foreign business person's point-of-view, what matters is understanding both versions and knowing when to refer to either version to avoid stepping on sensibilities. For example, when writing to a pro-independence Taiwanese business person, you would want to address the letter to "Taiwan" rather than to "Taiwan, Republic of China". On the other hand, if you are speaking with a Kuomingtang (Nationalist) government official, you would create much consternation by referring to the "Republic of Taiwan", as have several visiting European diplomats.

The Mainland Chinese Version in a Nutshell
Most of the Chinese (and their descendants) who retreated to Taiwan around 1949 to escape the communists view Taiwan as one of many provinces of China, albeit the only one controlled by the Republic of China (Nationalist) government. The civil war between the Nationalists and the Chinese Communist Party that began at the end of World War II still continues as a cold war. While hostilities on the battlefield have ended, the struggle between the communist People's Republic of China and the now democratic Republic of China on Taiwan remains intense. While many mainlanders in Taiwan have accepted the fact that Taiwan has become a de facto independent nation, many others hang on to the conviction that the Kuomintang (Nationalist) Party will someday return to mainland China and rule a unified China. These Kuomintang loyalists support the party's position that there is only one China and that it must someday be reunified.

The Taiwanese Version in a Nutshell
Many, if not most, of the Taiwanese who were on Taiwan prior to 1949 (and their descendants) view Taiwan as sufficiently different from mainland China as to be a separate political and cultural entity. While many Taiwanese acknowledge a shared Chinese cultural heritage with their cousins on the mainland, they still want their independence from China. Most favour the continued status quo separation from the mainland, or official independence. Those who favour the status quo say the risk of war with the People's

Republic of China, should Taiwan declare independence, is too great. Others favour an immediate declaration of independence and formation of a Republic of Taiwan.

Many Taiwanese feel they have been exploited by the mainland Nationalists. Others contend that the Nationalists invaded and colonised Taiwan. While the Taiwanese may mistrust the mainland Nationalists living among them, they have even less love for the communist People's Republic of China.

How Chinese is Taiwan?

This is not an easy question to answer. It is difficult to find reliable polling on the national identity of the residents of Taiwan. The little polling that has been conducted has been sponsored by the ROC government or pro-independence organisations and are, therefore, suspect. Ask the residents of the island of Taiwan if they are Chinese or Taiwanese and you will get a variety of answers. Most tend to identify themselves as "hyphenated Chinese"—in other words, as Taiwanese-Chinese. The vast majority will take pains to point out that their "Chinese-ness" has nothing to do with the People's Republic of China on the mainland. They despise the communist government in Beijing and want as little to do with it as possible. Most would like to get on with their lives and making a living—and let time and history solve the larger political issues.

BSRs and WSRs

The division between mainlanders and Taiwanese is exemplified by the code words used by the residents of Taiwan to label one another. Residents are either "BSRs" or "WSRs" depending on their arrival date. BSR stands for *Ben Shen Ren* or "Inside Province People" and literally means "native provincials". It refers to the people "originating" from Taiwan instead of mainland China. Most people believe that those who arrived in Taiwan before the 1945 ROC takeover are BSRs. Their offspring and those that arrived in Taiwan after 1945 are WSRs, which stands for *Wai Shen Ren* or "Outside

Province People". It means "visiting provincials". Their offspring are also considered WSRs, though marriages between BSRs and WSRs have blurred this classification.

Prospects for Unification with Mainland China

For diplomats and businesses around the world that wish the whole PRC-versus-Taiwan matter would just "go away", it does not look too promising. Many polls show that most Taiwan residents favour the status quo of undeclared independence. A ROC government-sponsored telephone poll in 1997 found that 35.4% of the respondents supported "keeping Taiwan's political status quo and letting everything be solved later". About 10% of the respondents favoured "Taiwan independence, as early as possible" and only 5.1% favoured "an early unification".

In the same poll, as many as 21.6% said "status quo forever" is the best policy, while 13.9% favoured "status quo for now and unification later". About 11.2% wanted "status quo for now and independence later". The poll was conducted by China Credit Information Service (CCIS) at the behest of the Mainland Affairs Council (MAC), the top ROC government agency in charge of Taiwan's mainland China policy.

Ilha Formosa

Taiwan was declared a protectorate of the Chinese Empire in 1206 and was subsequently ignored by the empire. In 1684, the island of Taiwan was made a county of the coastal Chinese province of Fujian. Taiwan officially became an integral part of the Chinese Empire when the Ching court conferred the status of *fu*, or prefecture, on the island in 1885. The island was then declared the twenty-second province of China.

For centuries, Taiwan was known to the non-Chinese world as Formosa, a name given to the island by 16th-century Portuguese explorers. On seeing the verdant island from their ships, the Portuguese named it Ilha Formosa or "beautiful island". While the

Portuguese named the island, the Chinese Empire ignored it and the Dutch coveted it.

The Dutch Period

The Dutch invaded Taiwan in 1624 and remained colonists for almost four decades. When they arrived to occupy Taiwan, they found only an aborigine population on the island. The Dutch brought in Chinese labourers as migrant workers. These labourers usually worked in Taiwan for a few years without their family before returning to mainland China. Eventually, many settled in Taiwan and married aborigine wives.

In 1662, the Dutch were driven out by Koxinga, also known as Cheng Cheng-kung, who was a Ming loyalist devoted to overthrowing the Ching government. He was forced to flee to Taiwan from the mainland after failing to recapture the Chinese capital of Nanjing from the Manchu invaders, who had usurped power and established the Ching dynasty. In Dutch-controlled Taiwan, Koxinga set about establishing a base for his struggle.

In Taiwan, Koxinga encountered the Dutch, who dismissed Koxinga as a mere pirate, incapable of mounting a serious threat. However, in 1662, they were defeated by Koxinga and forced to leave Taiwan. Koxinga became the ruler of Taiwan and gave the island its first formal Chinese government and turned it into a Ming outpost until his sudden death in 1663 at the age of 38. Koxinga's reign was brief but influential. He set up his court and government near Tainan and developed transportation and educational systems.

Koxinga's son and grandson ruled Taiwan until 1684, when the Ching finally succeeded in invading the island, snuffing out the last pocket of Ming resistance.

Today, in the southern city of Tainan, Koxinga's shrine sits in a garden of tropical trees and breezy pavilions. The shrine was built in 1875 by imperial edict from the Ching court in Beijing.

This was a landmark event. It indicated that the former Ming resistance leader was now forgiven and deified as a national hero.

The Nineteenth Century

The new Ching emperors did little to exercise control over remote Taiwan and it remained a frontier for the next 200 years. In the 1870s, Taiwanese pirates captured American, Japanese and French ships passing by the island. These foreign governments protested in Beijing but the Ching emperor replied that Taiwan was beyond his control.

In response, the French sent a fleet to the island and for nine months, from 1884 to 1885, Taiwan was a French territory. It was not until 1887, in response to Japanese moves to expand their power southward, that the Ching Imperial authorities decided to declare Taiwan a part of their empire. The flanking move by the Chinese did not stop the Japanese. In 1895, the Japanese defeated the Chinese in the Sino-Japanese War and in the Treaty of Shimonoseki, China ceded Taiwan to Japan in perpetuity.

The Taiwanese protested and declared the formation of the Republic of Taiwan, the first independent republic in Asia. The movement, however, was short-lived, as Japanese imperial troops crushed the movement within several months.

The Japanese Period

While the Japanese occupation was harsh, we cannot ignore the fact that Japan developed the island's infrastructure. The educational system was made similar to that in Japan. In addition, infrastructure (for example, roads), trains and industry were developed extensively.

In 1943, in the midst of World War II, the Allied powers agreed with Nationalist China's Chiang Kai-shek's statement that Taiwan would be "returned to (Nationalist) China". When the war ended in 1945, the Allied powers agreed that Nationalist Chinese troops would occupy Taiwan on behalf of the Allied forces. Most

Taiwanese were glad to get rid of the Japanese, but many felt uncomfortable with the ensuing influx of mainland Chinese who arrived as part of the occupying Nationalist Chinese forces.

After World War II

Tension between the Taiwanese and the mainlanders burst into the open in the February 28th Incident of 1947, when a small incident in Taipei—the authorities had arrested a woman selling cigarettes without a licence—sparked off large-scale public protests against repression and corruption. The Nationalist Chinese were surprised by the demonstrations and accused the Chinese communists and Japanese of fomenting the troubles. The Nationalists rounded up and executed many leading Taiwanese figures. In all, between 18,000 and 28,000 people were killed in the weeks following the February 28th Incident. Thousands of others were arrested and imprisoned in the "White Terror" campaign of the following decade. Many of them remained imprisoned until the early 1980s.

In 1949, the Nationalists lost the civil war on the mainland and fled to Taiwan where they established the remainder of their regime. For the next four decades, the people of Taiwan lived under martial law. The Chinese mainlanders who came over with Chiang Kai-shek constituted only 15% of the population of the island but were able to maintain themselves in a position of power over the native Taiwanese through tight control of the police, media and the political, military and educational systems.

Towards a Democratic and Independent Nation

The *tangwai* (outside the party) opposition started to question the Kuomintang's (KMT) anachronistic claim to represent all of China and began to demand an end to the 40-year-old martial law. In 1986, the Democratic Progressive Party (DPP) was founded. By the mid-1990s, the DPP had become a major opposition party and won several major city elections.

Martial law was lifted in 1987 and replaced by a less stringent National Security Law. However, it was not until 1991 that the KMT claim to rule all of China was dropped and the aging Nationalist Chinese legislators—elected on the mainland in 1947—were sent into retirement. Since then, Taiwan has made major strides in the direction of a fully democratic political system.

A Brief Economic History of Taiwan
Taiwan's economic growth rate averaged 6.42% per annum between 1953 and 1994, while per capita GNP rose from less than US$200 to nearly US$11,629 between 1952 and 1994. At the same time, the industrial segment of GDP rose from US$260 million to US$90 billion between 1951 and 1994. Taiwan's economic development since 1945 can be divided into six phases:

1940s: *Economic Reconstruction*
During the late 1940s, efforts were focused on building the infrastructure for the agricultural, industrial and transportation sectors. At the same time, the government implemented a land reform programme and initiated several large-scale projects to increase the productive output of textile, fertiliser and power plants. By the end of the 1940s, production of the island's agricultural, industrial, transportation and construction sectors had recovered to a level equal to the highest levels of the pre-World War II period.

1950s: *Development of Consumer Commodity Industries*
In the 1950s, Taiwan focused on a strategy of import substitution. First, agricultural productivity was promoted to supply the food processing industry. Then, the increased production of agriculture and its processed products was exported to earn foreign exchange for imports. In the meantime, manufacturers were encouraged to import lower value-added raw and semi-finished materials for production of higher value-added goods needed by the domestic market. During this period, yearly industrial growth averaged

11.7%, which made up almost two-thirds of an average economic growth rate of 7.6%.

1960s: *Rapid Growth of Light Industries*

In the 1960s, import substitution and export expansion continued to be major strategies. Manufacturing was vertically integrated to develop upstream components and parts. The local investment environment was improved and the government encouraged local manufacturers to export. The Statute for the Encouragement of Investment, which included tax holidays and credit incentives, became law and was actively promoted to multinational corporations. Many export processing zones were established to utilise the competitive advantage of lower labour costs.

As a result, during this period, exports increased at a dramatic average annual rate of 27.4%, paralleled by a 16.4% average increase in industrial output. In addition, the average yearly economic growth rate was pushed up to 10.2% and the commodity price index inflated by only 3.3% per year. Growth in the 1960s was not only rapid but stable, paving the way for future economic development.

1970s: *Development of Capital- and Technology-intensive Industries*

By the 1970s, the labour-intensive light industries' competitive advantage had peaked and the government realised that it had to move on to other industries to fuel the country's export engine. With abundant foreign exchange reserves, capital formation became easier for local industrialists. In addition to capital, technical labour and the expanded domestic market enabled the development of both capital- and technology-intensive industries such as the electronics and plastics industries.

In the late 1970s, the Ten National Construction Projects, which included the steel, shipbuilding, petrochemical, electricity, telecommunications and transportation industries, were completed one by one. These timely developments strengthened Taiwan's industrial structure and enabled the country to maintain a 14.1% average yearly increase in industrial output despite two energy crises and subsequent global recessions.

1980s: *Development of High-Tech Industries*
With the onset of the 1980s, the government began to focus on the strategic development of high-tech, high value-added and energy-efficient industries such as the computer, aerospace and telecommunications industries. The establishment of the Hsinchu Science-Based Industrial Park gave a boost to high-tech industries. Businesses were encouraged to intensify research and development while raising production capacity and quality to enhance competitiveness in the global marketplace. By 1990, high-tech products, mainly electronics, information and machinery products, accounted for 40.2% of total exports.

Meanwhile, the government tailored economic development policies to accommodate both domestic needs and international developments. Policies were implemented to create sustained economic growth, improve living standards and protect the environment with enhanced industrial pollution control measures. These measures were complemented by internationalisation and liberalisation measures, encouraging Taiwan companies to make structural adjustments and accelerate upgrading.

1990s: *Industrial Restructuring*
In recent years, industrial development has faced a number of heavy challenges, including the appreciation of the New Taiwan Dollar, wage increases, labour shortages, demands for better protection of the environment and competition from other developing countries. These factors have led to production facilities being moved offshore, as the competitive advantage that used to be enjoyed by low value-added, labour-intensive products was eliminated. To prevent the hollowing out of industry as traditional industries, such as the textiles and toys industries, move abroad,

structural adjustments must be made to raise the level of technology and speed up the development of new high-tech industries.

The government has promulgated the Six-year National Development Plan and the Statute for Upgrading Industries to accelerate the upgrading of industry so that Taiwan may incorporate itself into the society of developed nations by the year 2000. Infrastructure projects have been brought forward and tax incentives have been implemented. In addition, guidance and incentives have been provided for increased research and development, employee training, automation of production, pollution control and high-tech projects.

All these strategies are designed to enhance the competitiveness of traditional industries while providing an environment that will facilitate the development of the Ten Emerging Industries and attract the financial resources of both government and private investors to these promising new industries of the future.

Taiwan's Ministry of Economic Affairs estimates that the proportion of the traditional industries production to overall production will decline from 29.7% in 1994 to 25% in 2002. In contrast, the proportion of the production of the technology-

Ten Emerging Industries

- Telecommunications
- Information products
- Consumer electronics
- Semiconductors
- Precision machinery and automation
- Aerospace
- Advanced materials
- Fine chemicals and pharmaceuticals
- Healthcare
- Pollution control

intensive industries to overall production will increase from 34.1% to 40% in the same period, while that of basic industries, such as the steel and industrial machinery industries, will drop from 36.2% to 35%.

The Black Societies or Triads

Corporations, foreign or otherwise, involved in construction projects in Taiwan should be aware of the "black societies" of Taiwan and their organised crime ties. Secret societies or *hai dao bang pai* (black societies) have been part of Chinese history for thousands of years. They are big business in Taiwan.

Until the Anti-Hooligan Law authorising the arrest of triad members was passed in 1996, Taiwan's triads operated openly. The recognised "father" of the triads in Taiwan, Wolf Zhang, or "White Wolf", was a popular figure on television talk shows until the new law necessitated his move to mainland China. Zhang owns an investment business with many ventures in Taiwan and is still often called upon by business people to settle disputes.

Unlike Japan's yakuza, the triads of Taiwan do not have a strict rank and file. Businessmen and gangsters work side by side in most of the triads and both are members of the many *tongs* or subgroups that make up a triad. Each *tong* is led by a *da ge*, or big brother, who reports up the hierarchy and takes orders from the triad leadership.

Chapter 3

Dealing with the Government

Taiwan's government is actively involved in the island's economy. About a third of Taiwan's GDP is generated by state-owned enterprises. Taiwan's energy, banking, steel, insurance, salt, sugar, tobacco, beer and fertiliser industries are largely controlled by the central government. Chances are, if you are in any of these sectors, you will be dealing with the ROC government and/or the Kuomintang Party in some way.

Taiwan's bureaucrats devise and implement economic plans for the nation. The talented technocrats in Taiwan's government agencies utilise a flexible tax system, low-interest government loans and investment incentives to implement their economic plans.

The ROC Constitution

The Constitution of the Republic of China was promulgated on the mainland in 1947 before the ROC government retreated to Taiwan. No formal revisions to the constitution were made for over 40 years.

In 1991, the ROC government began to carry out constitutional revision based on changes in the external and domestic situation and to promote democracy. Martial law provisions were abolished and ten additional articles were appended to the constitution. These reformulated the manner of electing representatives to the National Assembly and the legislature, and the appointment of control yuan members.

The constitution has undergone four revisions during the 1990s. The objectives of the changes have been to streamline the government and provide for more democratic institutions. The latest round of revisions provided for the phasing out of the Taiwan provincial government, which is in line with the policy to eliminate the duplication of national and provincial government agencies.

Political Structure
The ROC government is divided into three main levels—central, provincial/municipal and county/city—each with well-defined powers. The central government consists of the Office of the President, the National Assembly and five governing branches, or yuans, namely the executive yuan, legislative yuan, judicial yuan, examination yuan and control yuan.

The Taiwan provincial government is split between the provincial level and the local level. At the provincial level, it exercises administrative responsibility and full jurisdiction over Taiwan's 16 counties and all Taiwanese cities, except Taipei and Kaohsiung. Taipei and Kaohsiung are special municipalities directly under the jurisdiction of the central government.

At the local level, the Taiwan provincial government consists of five city governments—Keelung, Hsinchu, Taichung, Chiayi

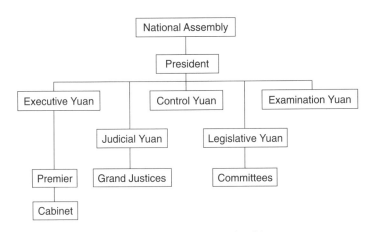

The Taiwanese Central Government Political Structure

and Tainan—and 16 county governments, with the governments of their subordinate cities and towns.

The National Government

In December 1949, following a civil war between the Communists and the ruling Nationalists, the People's Republic of China was founded on the mainland by the victorious communists. Chiang Kai-shek, the leader of the Nationalist Chinese regime, fled to the island of Taiwan that the Nationalists were already governing and established a "provisional" capital in Taipei.

From 1949 until 1991, the Nationalist Republic of China government on Taiwan claimed to be the sole legitimate governing body of all of China, including the mainland that they did not control. In keeping with that claim, when the Nationalists fled to Taiwan in 1949, they re-established the full array of central political bodies they had originally set up on the mainland. Taiwan province and later the special municipalities of Taipei and Kaohsiung were local bodies governed separately from the central administration. While this structure remains largely the same, the government on Taiwan has abandoned the claim of governing mainland China, stating that it does not "dispute the fact that the PRC controls mainland China".

The ROC government in Taipei exercises control over the islands of Taiwan, Kinmen, Matsu and the Penghu Islands. Taiwan's two major cities, Taipei and Kaohsiung, are administered as provincial-level municipalities. The rest of Taiwan and the Penghu Islands are administered together as Taiwan province. Kinmen and Matsu are administered by Taiwan authorities, but they are, in principle, considered to be part of the mainland province of Fujian.

Taiwan's national, or central, government consists of a president and vice-president elected directly by popular vote and five branches of government: the executive, legislative, judicial, examination and control yuans.

Lee Teng-hui was the first Taiwan-born president of the Republic of China on Taiwan.

President Lee Teng-hui

Taiwan's president was born 15 January 1923 at Sanchih, a small rural community on the outskirts of Taipei. After graduating from Taipei High School, he was admitted into Kyoto Imperial University in Japan and became part of a very small group of Chinese allowed to receive higher education during the Japanese occupation of Taiwan (1895–1945). After World War II, he returned home to continue his studies at National Taiwan University (NTU), majoring in agricultural economics. In 1951, Lee received a scholarship to study agricultural economics at Iowa State University in the United States. He returned to Taiwan with a master's degree and worked with the Provincial Department of Agriculture and Forestry while teaching part-time at NTU.

In 1957, Lee was transferred to the Chinese-American Joint Commission on Rural Reconstruction (JCRR). In 1970, he became chief of its Rural Economics Division. During his JCRR years, he made significant contributions to farmers' associations, irrigation systems, warehousing, rural health and farm mechanisation.

Lee served as a part-time professor of economics at NTU. Between 1958 and 1978, he also in the Graduate School of East Asian Studies at National Chengchi University in Taipei. In this period, Lee took three years' leave to pursue advanced studies at Cornell University and received his doctorate in agricultural economics in 1968. His thesis, "Intersectoral Capital Flows in the Economic Development of Taiwan", was cited as the best doctoral dissertation by the American Association for Agricultural Economics in 1969. In 1972, he was appointed minister without portfolio by Premier Chiang Ching-kuo and became the youngest person ever to hold such an office at the time. During his tenure, Lee was given the task of completing a five-year Vocational Training Programme, which ensured an adequate supply of trained manpower to meet the growing needs of industrialisation.

As mayor of Taipei (1978–1981), Lee improved administrative efficiency by expanding office automation and streamlining management procedures. He also initiated an annual music festival in 1979, setting a precedent for large-scale cultural activities sponsored by the government.

Lee was appointed governor of Taiwan Province in 1981. In this period, he concentrated on introducing regional planning techniques and a balanced development of urban and rural areas. He promoted rice crop substitution.

In 1984, he was elected vice-president and assisted the late President Chiang Ching-kuo in engineering various political and economic reforms. On the sudden death of President Chiang on 13 January 1988, Lee became president and completed the remainder of Chiang's term. On 20 March 1990, Lee was elected in his own right by the National Assembly as the eighth-term president of the Republic of China.

President Lee pushed through democratic reforms. He convened a National Affairs Conference in July 1990 as a forum for building up consensus on constitutional reform. Members of the parliament who had been in office for over four decades had to retire to make way for new candidates. Later, he proclaimed the end of martial law. Lee also presided over the passage of local self-government laws, the enactment of a constitutional amendment that ensured the direct election of the president and vice-president, and the completion of constitutional reform.

In 1990, Cornell University awarded Lee its first Outstanding International Alumnus Citation. In 1993, he was awarded the International Distinguished Achievement Citation by his alma mater—Iowa State University. In 1994, he was conferred the degree of Doctor of Laws honoris causa by Southern Methodist University of the United States.

Taiwan's first-ever direct presidential election took place on 23 March 1996. Lee won a landslide victory, garnering 54% of the votes and was sworn in as the ninth-term president of the Republic of China on 20 May 1996.

Even at a very young age, Lee showed great interest in literature, history and philosophy, and was especially attracted to the ideas of Immanuel Kant and Johann Wolfgang von Goethe. In recent years, he has been studying Chinese philosophy and Confucian humanism. His publications include *Agricultural and Economic Development in Taiwan* and *A Collection of Lee Teng-hui's Speeches* compiled by himself and published by his office. In 1949, Lee married Tseng Wen-fu. They have a son and two daughters.

The National Assembly

Under the constitution adopted by the KMT in 1947, the sovereignty of the people was to be exercised by the National Assembly. The first National Assembly was elected on the mainland in 1947 and was re-established in Taiwan when the KMT fled mainland China. The second National Assembly, elected in 1991, is composed of 325 members serving four-year terms.

The President

The president is the leader of Taiwan and commander-in-chief of its armed forces. As of 1996, the president is elected by direct vote of the people for a six-year term. In March 1996, Taiwan-born President Lee Teng-hui was elected by popular vote. With the consent of the legislative yuan, the president appoints the premier, who is the head of the executive yuan.

The Executive Yuan

The executive yuan is roughly analogous to the US executive branch of government in that it constitutes the cabinet and is responsible for policy and administration. The executive yuan includes the ministers of the various ministries and a few ministers without portfolio. Its members are nominated by the premier and appointed by the president. The premier leads the executive yuan.

The Legislative Yuan

The main lawmaking body is the legislative yuan, which has been in existence since the late 1940s. Originally viewed as a "rubber stamp" institution, the legislative yuan has, over time, greatly enhanced its standing in relation to the executive branch and has established itself as an important player on the central level.

The legislative yuan's main functions prior to August 1994 were to elect the president and vice-president and to amend the constitution. Amendments passed by the legislative yuan in July 1994 paved the way for direct election of the president and vice-president. Taiwan's first presidential election was held in March 1996. The legislative yuan's powers now include recalling the president and if necessary, impeaching the president, as well as ratifying certain presidential appointments in other branches of the government.

The legislative yuan has begun to reflect the recently liberalised political system. In the 1992 election, the main opposition party, the Democratic Progressive Party (DPP), challenged the KMT monopoly of the legislative yuan. In 1994, the legislative yuan passed legislation to allow for the direct election of certain local officials. In December 1995, the 164 members of the legislative yuan were elected to three-year terms (these members will be up for election in December 1998). While the results of this election did not give the opposition parties the majority they hoped for, the KMT found its majority in the council trimmed to only three seats. It managed to capture only 85 seats, its worst performance ever.

The Judicial Yuan

The judicial yuan administers Taiwan's court system. It includes a 17-member Council of Grand Justices that interprets the constitution. Grand justices are appointed by the president—with the consent of the National Assembly—to nine-year terms.

The Examination Yuan

The examination yuan functions as a civil service commission. It is responsible for the examination, employment and management of all civil service personnel. This council oversees the screening and qualification standards for civil servants, as well as their retirement benefits.

The primary reason for the examination yuan's existence as a separate government branch from the executive branch is so that it is free from partisan influence.

> **ROC Web Page**
> The ROC government maintains a useful website that lists the
> ROC government officials and their posts. The site can be
> accessed at http://www.taipei.org/info/chief/index_e.html

The Control Yuan

The control yuan monitors the efficiency of the public service
and investigates instances of corruption. The 29 control yuan
members are appointed by the president and approved by the
National Assembly. They serve six-year terms. Recently, the
control yuan has become more active and has conducted several
major investigations and impeachments.

The Ministries

The Ministry of Economic Affairs (MOEA)

This mega-agency is responsible for managing the country's
economic policy and its implementation. In other words, it is
responsible for Taiwan's long-term development. The MOEA's
scope of functions encompasses industry, commerce, trade, energy
and mining. The foreign business executive will find the MOEA
to be ubiquitous within the business realm of Taiwan.

Taiwan's economic management responsibility was not always
as concentrated as it is today. When the ROC constitution was
promulgated in 1947, economic matters were the responsibility
of three ministries—industry and commerce, agriculture and
forestry, and water conservancy—and one commission (resources)
under the executive yuan. When the government moved to Taipei
in 1949, the three ministries were combined to form the Ministry
of Economic Affairs in order to simplify administration and improve
focus. In 1952, the resources commission was also merged with
the MOEA; the state corporations that had been part of the
resources commission were transferred to the MOEA. In 1981,

the MOEA transferred securities management to the Ministry of Finance and took over the responsibility of the salt enterprise from the Ministry of Finance (MOF). In 1984, the MOEA unloaded its agricultural responsibilities on the Council of Agriculture.

The MOEA comprises 16 staff units, 13 administrative agencies, seven national corporations and 59 overseas commercial offices. If you have ever dealt with the commercial staff of Taiwan's overseas embassies or consulates (official or unofficial), you have probably dealt with MOEA staff.

The 13 administrative agencies in the MOEA include the:

- Board of Foreign Trade
- Bureau of Commodity Inspection and Quarantine
- Central Geological Survey
- Commission of National Corporations
- Energy Commission
- Export Processing Zone Administration
- Industrial Development Bureau
- International Economic Cooperation Development Fund
- International Trade Commission
- Investment Commission
- National Bureau of Standards
- Professional Training Centre
- Small and Medium Business Administration
- Water Resources Planning Commission

The state enterprises operated by the MOEA include the:

- China Shipbuilding Corporation
- Chinese Petroleum Corporation
- Taiwan Fertiliser Company
- Taiwan Machinery Manufacturing Corp.
- Taiwan Power Company
- Taiwan Salt Works
- Taiwan Sugar Corporation

The Price Control Commission of the MOEA sets price controls for the products and services of most of the state-owned enterprises. Petroleum, sugar and utilities are subject to price control. The Commodity Price Supervisory Board, which consists of representatives from the MOF, MOEA, central bank, the Agriculture Commission and the Ministry of Communications, monitors prices closely.

The Ministry of Finance

The MOF is responsible for supervising Taiwan's financial markets and institutions. Through its Bureau of Monetary Affairs, the Securities and Exchange Commission and the Department of Insurance, the MOF regulates Taiwan's financial system. The MOF also formulates the financial policies of the nation and promotes the development of the financial services industry in Taiwan.

The nine departments of the MOF include the following:

- National Treasury
- Taxation
- Customs Administration
- Insurance
- General Affairs
- Personnel Affairs
- Anti-corruption
- Accounting
- Statistics

The major functions of the MOF are the maintenance of the national treasury, the customs and tariff system, and the taxation system. It also regulates the insurance and banking industries. The responsibilities of the MOF are as follows:

National Treasury

- To enforce fiscal policies and maintain a balanced budget
- To raise construction funds to meet the needs of the economic development of the country
- To regulate public treasury systems and supervise the treasury administration at all levels of the government
- To adjust revenues and expenditures and secure economic stability through government debt policy

Taxation

- To design tax policies and the taxation system, and to supervise the collection of taxes and duties at all levels of tax offices
- To improve the tax structure and the distribution of tax burden
- To establish an overall sound tax environment to meet the needs of economic development

Customs Administration

- To devise customs policy and plan tariff systems
- To set and review import tariff rates, classification of products and customs valuation
- To enact customs and anti-smuggling regulations
- To supervise customs administration in clearance, duty drawback and bonding systems
- To handle international customs affairs

Insurance

- To revise the Insurance Law and related regulations in order to cope with economic development
- To ensure the solvency of each insurer to protect the interests of policy holders
- To establish a sound insurance market by supervising and regulating the operations of insurers
- To educate the general public in the field of insurance

Banking
- To establish a sound money market, to apply financial policy and measures, and to support the development of the agricultural, industrial and commercial sectors
- To promote economic development by providing proper financial laws and regulations
- To establish a sound financial system by governing and supervising the operation of banks and other financial institutions

Securities and Futures Administration
- To enlarge the scale of the issuance market to meet the needs of enterprises
- To establish a sound trading market to safeguard investors' interests
- To ensure full disclosure of financial statements by supervising the operation of CPAs
- To supervise foreign futures trading and to establish a domestic futures market

National Property
- Takeover and registration of national land
- Management of national real estate not for public use
- Disposal of national real estate not for public use
- Development of national real estate not for public use

Ministry of Transportation and Communication
The Ministry of Transportation and Communications is charged with the administration of all transportation and communications operations and enterprises in Taiwan. The ministry consists of three functional departments—Railways and Highways, Posts and Telecommunications, and Aviation and Navigation—as well as other departments, offices and committees that are responsible

for formulating policy, laws and regulations, and overseeing operations in the area of transportation and communications.

Transportation and communications operations are divided into four categories: communications, transportation, meteorology and tourism.

Communications operations encompass the posts and telecommunications department. The postal section comes under the control of the Directorate General of Posts, while the telecommunications section is administered by the Directorate General of Telecommunications and managed by Chunghwa Telecom Company.

Transportation operations are divided into land, sea and air transportation. Land transportation comprises railway (including highspeed rail and general rail) and highway transportation, as well as mass rapid transit systems. Highspeed rail is planned and sponsored by the Bureau of Taiwan Highspeed Rail. General rail, highway transportation and mass rapid transit systems are operated by provincial and city governments, and private companies, while freeways are managed and maintained by the Taiwan Area National Freeway Bureau and constructed by the Taiwan Area National Expressway Engineering Bureau.

Air transportation includes airline companies and airports. Airline companies are privately operated, while airports and flight navigation services are under the control of the Civil Aeronautics Administration.

Sea transportation consists of marine shipping companies and harbours. Marine shipping companies are either operated by government agencies or private corporations. All harbours are operated by the various harbour bureaus under the Taiwan provincial government.

This ministry also oversees the Central Weather Bureau, which handles all national meteorological operations, and the Tourism Bureau, which provides for planning and oversight of tourism development.

The following agencies are part of the Ministry of Transportation and Communications:

- Central Weather Bureau
- Directorate General of Posts
- National Freeway Bureau
- Directorate General of Telecommunications
- Tourism Bureau
- Civil Aeronautics Administration
- Marine Meteorology Centre
- National Expressway Engineering Bureau
- Institute of Transportation
- Professional Office of High Speed Rail
- Chunghwa Telecom
- Aeronautical Training Centre, CAA, MOTC
- Engineering Office of Taipei Railway Underground Project

Ministry of the Interior

The Ministry of the Interior consists of 10 departments, two offices and four agents. Outlined below are the departments that might be relevant to your business.

Department of Civil Affairs   In charge of administration and autonomy of local governments, frontier administration management of public properties, civic organisations, elections, religion, ceremony and customs, funeral and memorial services, sacrificial rites and other civil affairs.

Department of Population   In charge of household registration, nationality administration, population policy, issuance of identification cards, emigration planning and other population administrative affairs.

Department of Social Affairs In charge of social welfare, social insurance, social relief, community development, social services, rehabilitation of handicapped citizens, civic organisations and other social administrative affairs.

Department of Land Affairs In charge of land survey and registration, land value assessment, equalisation of land rights, land entitlements investigation, land reclamation, compulsory acquisition of land, land utilisation, territorial administration and other land administrative affairs.

Ministry of National Defence

Companies trying to do business with the armed forces of Taiwan should realise that the Ministry of Defence in Taiwan does not wield as much power as in most countries. The Ministry of Defence only gets 5% of the annual defence budget, while the armed forces general staff receive 70% of the US$9 billion-plus budget. The ministry can do little more than try to persuade the military to make wise purchase decisions.

Taiwan's military operates as an independent agency over which there is very little control. The chief of the general staff has to answer only to the president who, critics charge, is too busy to pry deeply into the military's affairs. During the 1990s, the armed forces was rocked by allegations of corruption in bid-rigging and construction projects. Corruption had become so rife by 1998 that both the president and the legislative yuan were considering new legislation to bring accountability to the military.

Military

Taiwan maintains a large military establishment. Its primary mission is defence of Taiwan predominantly from the PRC, which has steadfastly refused to renounce the use of force against Taiwan. It is widely believed that the PRC would attack Taiwan if the island declares official independence. This is why most Taiwanese prefer to maintain the current ambiguousness of their status as a de facto independent nation.

Because of the threat from the formidable military might of the PRC, Taiwan has maintained a large and potent military force since the 1960s. The ROC military includes the army, navy (includes marines), air force, coastal patrol and defence command, armed forces reserve command and combined service forces. In 1997, Taiwan ranked 11th in the world in military expenditures (US$11.14 billion) and 15th in the number of military personnel employed (425,000).

Since 1990, Taiwan's military spending has increased slightly in real terms, while the number of personnel has decreased. This is due to the military's increased reliance on advanced technology. Taiwan's focus is on developing an indigenous military manufacturing capability, producing a variety of high technology weapons, including fighter aircraft.

Although Taiwan tries to produce more of its own weaponry, it cannot manufacture all the defensive weapons it needs. The country is the world's third largest importer of arms, importing US$1.2 billion of equipment in 1997 alone. Only Saudi Arabia and Egypt import more arms. Taiwan imports most of its military hardware from the United States and France. It is, in fact, working with the United States to develop a more advanced naval force. Taiwan shows no intention of developing a force other than for defensive reasons.

The Council of Agriculture (COA)
The COA is part of the executive yuan, or Cabinet. It is in charge of policies and programmes for agriculture, forestry, food, fishing and animal husbandry. It oversees the relevant provincial and municipal government programmes but leaves day-to-day implementation in the hands of the local governments.

Local Governments

County and city governments play an important role in Taiwan, independent from the provincial government. There are 16 counties and county governments in Taiwan, which consist of councils with city mayors and county magistrates who are elected by direct vote of the citizenry for four-year terms.

China External Trade Association (CETRA)

The China External Trade Development Council (CETRA) was founded in 1970 to promote Taiwan's foreign trade. Over the past quarter of a century, CETRA has become Taiwan's foremost non-profit trade promotion organisation, providing comprehensive trade-related services to the domestic and foreign business communities. CETRA is jointly sponsored by the government and industrial and commercial associations.

CETRA has offices throughout the world that act as research posts for Taiwan's businesses. CETRA makes information and analysis available via publications (primarily in the Chinese language) and a large trade library that has branches in Taipei, Taichung, Tainan and Kaohsiung. CETRA's trade library at its Taipei headquarters is one of the best in the world. Business-related magazines from many countries—from Argentina to Vietnam—and 12 computer databases are available for the admission price of about US$3.

Whether you are researching markets in Taiwan or other countries, CETRA's libraries should not be overlooked. Most of CETRA's original research is available only in Chinese, but there is a large collection of reference materials available in English. Everything from market information, import/export product catalogues, trade directories and tariff schedules to trade laws and market research is available in English.

CETRA's English publications include *Taiwan Trade Opportunities*, a monthly bulletin that outlines trade opportunities, business news and listings of export and import inquiries, and *Taiwan Products*, a series of slick, full-colour publications that focus on different industrial sectors and their products in each issue—for example, auto parts or bicycles. CETRA also publishes a Chinese-language daily newspaper called *Trader's Express*.

The Taipei Venture Capital Association (TVCA)

The leadership of Taiwan recognises that science and technology is a major driving force for the country's continued economic growth. As the manufacturing of lower-technology products gradually moves to lower-cost labour markets, such as Vietnam, Taiwan seeks to replace the loss with higher value-added products. The government is, therefore, planning to do what it can to steer the private sector in this direction.

To motivate the private sector to increase Research and Development (R&D) investment, the government now provides direct subsidies for R&D to key areas in the private sector. At the same time, to help finance this development, TVCA, a private sector association, began a programme in 1996 to channel local venture capital from traditional industries, such as heavy manufacturing and petrochemicals, into high technology industries. This programme also encouraged collaboration with both Japan and the United States. TVCA works with foreign high-tech firms that seek capital in Taiwan or sell technology to Taiwan.

Accessibility of Taiwan's Market

This topic has been included here as market access is largely a matter of the degree of access allowed by the ROC government.

Taiwan has been increasing the level of foreign access to its market because of the ROC government's drive to make Taiwan a regional operations centre and a member of the World Trade Organisation (WTO). In conjunction with this drive to internationalise and liberalise its markets, Taiwan has revised its customs laws and reduced tariffs, as well as the number of products that require import licences. Taiwan has also reduced restrictions on foreign investment and developed new incentives to encourage investments in certain sectors.

Tariffs and Import Barriers

The bad news is that Taiwan, like the People's Republic of China (PRC), levies import taxes in the forms of both value-added taxes (VAT) and tariffs. The good news is that tariffs are lower in Taiwan than in China. The country has made significant progress in reducing tariffs on non-agricultural products since 1995. Taiwan has also agreed to abide by the WTO customs valuation code.

Importers in Taiwan must pay a 5% VAT and a 0.5% harbour construction fee. A commodity tax must also be paid if an imported item falls into certain commodity categories. Rates range from 2%–60% on a few high-value or luxury products, such as automobiles, jewellery and liquor. Taiwan's high tariffs are designed to discourage importation and thus encourage the purchase of local substitutes. For example, the average nominal duty for automotive parts is 20%, while the current actual duty rate for passenger cars is 30% and that for commercial vehicles is 35%–42%. However, the effective rate (duty plus taxes) for passenger cars and trucks is 60%–100%.

Many agricultural tariffs were lowered as part of Taiwan's 1995 unilateral tariff reductions. Nevertheless, foreign firms trying to import their products into Taiwan consider many of the reduced tariffs, as well as other agricultural tariffs, to be high enough to create a significant barrier. Some examples include fresh fruit (40%–42%), processed vegetables, including vegetable juices (35%–40%), and sunflower seeds and oil (21%–24%).

In addition, a 1997 report by the US trade representative's office reported that US agricultural exporters have increasingly reported instances in which Taiwanese customs authorities have reclassified import items to categories with higher tariffs, often after years of trade history. This practice is most prominent in agricultural commodities, such as mixed feed stuffs, tallow and grease, and intermediate ingredients.

Exporters who have sold to China will find that Taiwan has significantly fewer non-tariff trade barriers than China. However, Taiwan still has non-tariff barriers and continues to maintain an import licensing system, albeit one in which the number of items that require import licences is gradually being reduced.

Government Procurement Practices

Non-transparent bidding procedures continue to hinder foreign firms from bidding on major projects in Taiwan. In those cases where the Central Trust of China (CTC), a ROC government-owned trust bank, administers the procurement programme, the record of foreign bidders' success is good. The trust takes pains to adhere to international and WTO standards by giving foreign firms a fair opportunity to win bids. However, most government purchases are administered by the purchasing entities themselves, not the CTC. The record in these projects is not favourable to foreign firms.

Although government procurement is usually administered by the government entity making the purchase, any central government agency can authorise the CTC as an agent to make purchases for it and is required to use this public enterprise for purchases over NT$50 million. In such cases, CTC is authorised to solicit foreign tenders. The Ministry of Defence, government educational institutes and government-owned enterprises may conduct their own foreign procurement without the CTC.

Many tenders are restricted to firms with local presence. The Industrial Development Bureau of the Ministry of Economic Affairs administers a "Buy Domestic Policy" and "Industrial Cooperation Programme" to help domestic suppliers win government procurement contracts. Therefore, foreign firms should have a local office or a representative/agent in Taiwan. Without local presence, it is also very difficult for foreign firms to obtain advance notice on upcoming bids. There are short windows of opportunity to submit bids on many projects. Without advance warning, it is difficult to submit successful bids on time.

Intellectual Property Rights

Taiwan is still developing a mature legal system and is making progress in improving protection of intellectual property (IP) and its enforcement. Since 1992, a series of important IP laws have been passed, including revised copyright, patent and trademark laws. If new legislation under consideration to protect integrated circuit designs and trade secrets is passed, Taiwan will have an Intellectual Property Rights (IPR) legal structure largely consistent with international practices.

Piracy remains a problem in Taiwan. According to a 1998 US report, Taiwan remains one of the top four sources of pirated goods seized by the US customs. It is also a major source of similar illegal exports to Latin American markets, especially Paraguay. The authorities have improved their enforcement efforts, but inconsistencies in the trademark and patent area emphasise the need for more standardised examination and registration procedures. Successful prosecutions have been mounted in the area of computer hardware and software, and in the area of films and music.

The authorities have focused on stamping out computer hardware and software piracy, in part to protect its own large information technology (IT) industry from retaliation by other countries. The Ministry of the Interior and the Ministry of Economic Affairs' Anti-counterfeiting Committee have worked to root out copyright infringements in the IT and entertainment industries. All computer software, hardware and compact discs exported from Taiwan require export permits. Inspections of outbound software shipments have been stepped up in an effort to stop exports of pirated products.

More information about Taiwan's copyright law and regulations is available from the Ministry of the Interior. The ministry maintains an English language web page that contains a complete translation of copyright laws and regulations, as well as information on how firms can engage in copyright dispute mediation with other firms.

Applying for a Patent in Taiwan
Patent applications should be sent to the National Bureau of Standards' Patents Office in Taipei. The application must be submitted in Chinese and include, among other things, a petition that states the full particulars of the patent, a certificate of the applicant's nationality and specifications describing the nature and uses of the invention. All this must be done through an authorised patent attorney of Taiwanese nationality.

Copyright Protection
Foreign authors must publish their works in Taiwan in order to be able to register and claim protection for the works. Works by Hong Kong, Swiss, British and US nationals are entitled to automatic protection. Copyrights must be registered with the Copyright Committee of the Ministry of the Interior.

Foreign Investment in Taiwan

Transparency in Foreign Investment
Taiwan has actively used foreign investment incentives to attract investors in desired sectors of the economy. Taiwan has also established three export processing zones that facilitate foreign investment and export. Many foreign manufacturers import components duty-free into these zones for processing by Taiwan's skilled labour force. They then re-export the finished products to other countries.

Potential foreign investors must submit an application for screening and approval (or disapproval) by the ROC government. The screening process is nondiscriminatory in Taiwan for those sectors open to foreign investment. A few sectors, such as television networks, are closed to foreign investment in varying degrees. The regulations change periodically, but the current sectors that are closed to foreign investment are explicitly listed as such by the ROC government.

The restrictions on foreign investment that are in place are generally transparent. The "negative list" that Taiwan maintains clearly specifies industries closed to foreign investment and where foreign ownership is limited.

Difficulties with local authorities and citizen groups over environmental protection are, however, becoming increasingly common. For example, when Formosa Plastics tried to build a sixth naphtha cracker in Taiwan in the mid-1990s, the strong environmentalist movement on the island successfully lobbied for denial of construction permits.

Government Attitudes Toward Foreign Investment in Taiwan

Taiwan authorities are well aware of the fact that the island's competitiveness as a manufacturing site for foreign corporations has declined. Lower cost alternatives have arisen in Indonesia, Malaysia and elsewhere in East and Southeast Asia. Indeed, much of Taiwan's own manufacturing base has shifted to these markets.

To offset the decline in the manufacturing sector, the government has shifted its investment strategy to focus on attracting foreign suppliers of financial services and portfolio capital to Taiwan.

Government Influence on Outbound Investment

Foreign countries interested in attracting Taiwanese investments used to head straight to the ROC government to display their wares. With the spread of democracy in Taiwan, foreigners have learned that the ROC government no longer has the power to tell Taiwanese companies where to invest. The authorities in Taipei have been somewhat slow to realise this.

In 1993, Taipei announced a "Go South" policy, calling on Taiwan's corporations to step up their investments in Southeast Asia rather than in mainland China. While Taiwanese corporations have invested US$37 billion in Association of Southeast Asian Nations (ASEAN) countries, the programme has failed to reach any of its goals. Taiwanese companies have continued to focus on opportunities in China and North America. Even as Taipei re-launched its "Go South" policy in 1998—in the midst of the Southeast Asian financial crisis—Taiwanese companies were scrambling to downgrade their investments in the region.

Obtaining Investment Permits
The application procedure for foreign investors is relatively straightforward. Investors first have to obtain an application form from the Department of Commerce at the Ministry of Economic Affairs (MOEA), to which they will later submit the completed form stating their company name in order to establish the legitimacy of the chosen company name.

The application forms are in Chinese but may be accompanied by translated versions if required. Applications are usually processed within two to three weeks. After obtaining approval, investors can remit their capital, register the company, begin construction if necessary and apply to local authorities for water and electricity.

Chapter 4

The Business Environment

A Unique Environment—A Blend of Confucianism and Western Ways

---

The Taiwanese Way

"I had over a decade of experience in the People's Republic of China, so my company assigned me to open their new Taiwan office. They thought that I knew how to operate in the "Chinese world" of business. What both my company and I failed to realise was that Taiwan is a unique hybrid of traditional Chinese Confucian culture and Western culture. This is a doubly confusing place for expatriates to do business because we never know whether to do things the "Chinese way" or the "Western way". The only answer is to learn the "Taiwanese way".

— A British expatriate in Taipei

While the business environment of Taiwan shares similarities with the other "Tigers" of East and Southeast Asia and with the rest of "Greater China", the island is a market unto itself. This uniqueness is evident by the criticisms (and occasional reluctant praises) aimed at Taiwan by the mainland Chinese, the Singaporeans, the Koreans and people from other Asian countries. The degree to which a group is criticised by its neighbours serves as a barometer of both the neighbours' intolerance and the singular culture of those being criticised.

Mainland Chinese business people often express dismay at the "rudeness" and "brusqueness" of their Taiwanese counterparts. The perception of Taiwanese as being rude seems to stem from the pace with which they conduct business. The Taiwanese tend

83

to focus on getting the business done at all costs while the mainlanders are more bureaucratic and, thus, slower paced in business. The mainlanders resent the lack of attention Taiwanese pay to building a business relationship. Anyone operating in both the PRC and Taiwan markets should heed these differences in the business environment.

Taiwanese are viewed as shrewd, no-nonsense business people by their neighbours. They are sometimes accused of exploiting less developed markets but everyone, including their rivals in Beijing, hungers for Taiwan's investments and copies their successful business systems. For decades, Korea looked on Taiwan's devotion to developing small and medium-sized businesses with derision. In contrast, the Korean governments favoured and protected a few large conglomerates in the country. The Asian Financial Crisis of 1988 hit Korea's giant conglomerates hard, while Taiwan's lean and flexible companies helped the country get through the crisis largely unscathed.

The Japanese Influence

The Japanese influence on the business practices of Taiwan cannot be ignored. During the Japanese occupation of Taiwan from 1895 to 1945, Tokyo tried to assimilate Taiwan into the Japanese Empire. Throughout these 50 years, the Japanese developed the economy of Taiwan, instituted a Japanese-style educational system and exposed the Taiwanese to the Japanese industrial system. Those Taiwanese who were schooled prior to 1945 were taught Japanese.

During its occupation of Taiwan, Japan built roads, railroads and other infrastructure that survived World War II and gave the Taiwanese a foundation upon which to develop. Their exposure to the very successful Japanese way of business during the colonial period was also of benefit to the entrepreneurs of postwar Taiwan. The existing infrastructure, combined with Taiwanese business acumen, enabled them to fully utilise postwar American aid. The rising class of Taiwanese business people and company founders were also able to use their knowledge of Japanese practices to win business deals with the Japanese in the 1960s and 1970s.

Corruption Taiwan-style

Corruption is as old as civilisation itself and no country is without some form of it. Taiwan is no exception. Both the Taiwanese and foreign business people agree that corruption is a much bigger problem in Taiwan today than it was 10 or 20 years ago. An alarming number of Taiwan's elected officials have criminal links. Even the government estimates that about 10% of the national legislature, 20% of the provincial legislature and over 30% of the county officials have ties to triads and other criminal groups.

The average foreign business person doing business in Taiwan need not worry about corruption, but when dealing in large projects, especially infrastructure projects, the underside of Taiwanese commercial life will likely get in your way. Most of the bribery, threats and other nefarious forms of corruption originate within the Chinese triads and organised crime gangs. Connections between Taiwan's local politicians (city, county, provincial) and organised crime are not uncommon.

The Black Societies and Commercial Corruption

Taiwan's authorities have tried to fight organised crime in the country but seem to be fighting a very difficult war. The passage of tough anti-organised crime legislation in the mid-1990s has given the police greater authority and recent crackdowns have forced some of the leaders of Taiwan's organised crime brotherhood to flee to mainland China.

Most of the island's organised crime is controlled by the *hai dao bang pai* (black societies) or triads, which are endemic in many Chinese societies. Most of these secret societies have their roots as honourable patriotic organisations. Over time, they became wealthy empires involved in criminal activities. Gambling, prostitution and loan-sharking have been the foundation of the triads' business empires.

The triads were founded in the late 17th century by ethnic Han Chinese for the purpose of repelling the invading Manchus and restoring the imperial throne to China's Ming dynasty. The triad was derived from a symbolic equilateral triangle, each side representing the concepts of Heaven, Earth and man. The implication was that, with the backing of the harmonious triangle, patriotic efforts against the invading foreigner (in this case, the Manchus of Manchuria) would succeed.

The triads, however, did not succeed. Instead, the Manchu force crushed the few pockets of Ming resistance in southern China and forced the triads underground. Deprived of much needed support from local populations, the triads turned to criminal activities like piracy, smuggling, prostitution and extortion for survival. By the 1900s, most triads had abandoned their patriotic raison d'etre and were fully engrossed in the highly profitable criminal businesses. In the later half of the 20th century, the triads had modernised and expanded into mainstream businesses like waste disposal and construction.

Triads, such as the notorious United Bamboo, learned that real money was to be made in rake-offs or illegal commissions from public works projects. The triads then decided to force their way into these deals and join forces with unscrupulous politicians and construction conglomerates that had been rigging bids on these multi-million dollar infrastructure projects for years. Some estimates put the rake-offs on these projects as high as 30% of the total bids. During one six-year period in the 1990s, US$26 billion was estimated to have been siphoned off public works projects by Taiwan's triads and politicians. Some in the industry say that a 50% built-in profit margin is the average for winning bids in Taiwan's public works projects.

Many foreign firms in the construction industry have shied away from playing in the Taiwan market. This is because their unwillingness to pay kickbacks makes them lose out on contracts. If lucky, these foreign firms end up working as subcontractors on very thin profit margins. Legitimate local builders are often shut out of public works projects. Some Taiwanese builders restrict their work to small projects that the triads consider unprofitable.

Corruption in public projects and in the re-zoning of land for construction are common at the county level. The potential pay-offs in projects at this level are so immense that many of the county commissioner's seats have been bought by triad members. Once in office, the commissioner can mete out infrastructure contracts at any price he or she likes. Word is that 5% kickbacks are the average on county contracts. Foreign businesses bidding on projects at the county level should consult local partners.

Also of potential interest to foreign companies doing business here is the practice some Taiwan companies have of using triads to arbitrate commercial disputes. The triads have the knack of moving quickly to collect debts, more so than the slow judicial process. Even publicly listed corporations turn to the triads to help them get the necessary votes in proxy fights. Corporations are also known to hire triad-owned security guard firms to keep "uppity" stockholders in line at annual meetings.

Graft related to government projects will not end until the bidding system is made more transparent. Foreign contractors are barred from bidding on most government projects and are allowed to participate only in a few "international tenders".

Business and the Law

The foreign business person must be aware of Taiwanese law and should see expert advice. However, it is more important to be familiar with Taiwanese attitudes to the law. As you learn about Taiwan's legal system, keep in mind that legal niceties aside, the Taiwanese take a flexible approach to their system. Legal relationships can be varied as circumstances change and as dictated by the need to avoid conflict.

The business society in Taiwan is not orderly. If placed on a scale with the German's "Order must prevail" approach on one end and the Thai's "It can't be helped" approach on the other, Taiwan would be decidedly towards the Thai end of the spectrum. Taiwanese business people often maintain that anything not specifically outlawed is encouraged. The rule of law, at least as it is applied to commercial law, is still being developed in Taiwan.

Taiwan's jurisprudence differs in many important respects from that of its neighbours. The legal system borrows heavily from the German system; the law is based on a code rather than a series of statutes and precedents. The Taiwanese do not base legal decisions on precedents, preferring to treat each case as a new one to be decided on its own merits. Commercial law in Taiwan has developed rapidly by largely adopting from Western commercial law.

Taiwan's supreme law is the ROC's constitution. The legislative yuan enacts and amends the Civil Code that largely governs business relationships in the country. The legislative yuan also enacts statutes and regulations to amend the legal system.

Foreign lawyers cannot operate legal practices in Taiwan but may set up consulting firms or work with local law firms. Qualified foreign attorneys may act as consultants to Taiwan law firms and provide legal advice to their employers.

Board of Foreign Trade

The Ministry of Economic Affairs' Board of Foreign Trade (BOFT) advises the government on trade policies, promotes the development of trade and maintains statistics on Taiwan's external trade. BOFT is the workhorse that manages Taiwan's participation in regional economic organisations like the Asia Pacific Economic Conference (APEC). This is where the nation's trade policies are formulated and implemented.

BOFT will interest foreign companies that need trade statistics. A visit to the BOFT headquarters in Taipei can garner reams of useful industry- or market-specific trade data. Companies can use BOFT data to find out where Taiwan's exports are headed—even down to the individual states in some countries. Most of this information is still available only on hard copy.

The Commercial Registration Act

The Commercial Registration Act of Taiwan requires that all companies doing business in Taiwan be registered or licensed to do business. Once registered, the company may do business in Taiwan but only within the scope of business for which it has been registered. The form and operation of business in Taiwan is controlled by the Civil Code of Taiwan as well as the statutes passed by the legislative yuan.

Legal Forms of Business

Taiwan's legal system allows for four kinds of company organisation:

- Unlimited company
- Limited company
- Unlimited company with limited liability shareholders
- Company limited by shares

The unlimited company is one that is organised by two or more shareholders who bear unlimited and joint liability of the obligations of the company. The limited company is one organised by not less than five or more than 21 shareholders who are liable to the extent of the capital subscribed by them.

Trademarks and Patents

Counterfeiting of famous name products has decreased but remains a problem. Taiwan's enforcement of intellectual property protection was lax for many years, but the situation improved in the mid-1990s. Not coincidentally, the authorities began to crack down on piracy in Taiwan at the same time that the country's high-tech industries began to suffer from competition from pirated goods. In 1995, Taiwan passed laws to protect integrated circuit layouts, personal data and trade secrets. In 1997, two much-needed intellectual property rights (IPR) laws were enacted by Taiwan's legislature. As a result, Taiwan's IPR legal structure is now largely consistent with the WTO Agreement on Trade-Related Aspects of Intellectual Property Rights.

Improved enforcement efforts, including an export monitoring system for computer software and trademarked goods, have reduced piracy. In 1996, Taiwan announced an "Action Plan" to strengthen its domestic enforcement and crackdown on domestic firms involved in compact disc (CD) piracy in mainland China. Taiwan's CD manufacturing firms began to place specific identification codes on their products

Trademark protection is available to foreign individuals and corporations doing business in Taiwan. The protection extends to internationally famous trademarks even if the foreign owner has not registered the trademark in Taiwan, but this applies only if the relevant foreign country does the same for Taiwanese corporations. Taiwan, in accordance with international legal customs, usually reciprocates protections offered to its citizens by foreign governments. Foreign businesses should, however, note that protection in most instances is granted on the basis of priority of registration and not priority of use. It is, therefore, essential that foreign corporations register their trademarks in Taiwan as soon as possible.

Patents

Applications for patents are handled by MOEA's National Bureau of Standards. An inventors or his/her assignees must submit a written application to the bureau. If an application is approved, it is published in the bureau's *Patent Gazette* and is effective immediately upon publication. In Taiwan, patent rights last five years for new designs, 10 years for a new utility model and 15 years for a new invention.

Licensing Laws and Technical Cooperation Projects

Licensing agreements in Taiwan are generally straightforward. Firms pay royalties or service fees for the right to use technologies, trademarks or patents. Since 1995, royalties paid have been subject to Taiwan's income tax, but only foreign companies and their subsidiaries incorporated in Taiwan are subject to ROC corporate income tax. As with all tax-related matters, consult an accountant and/or attorney for updates on legal matters.

Since 1995, Taiwan has not required that parties to an international licensing agreement obtain approval from MOEA's Foreign Investment Commission (FIC) to enter into such agreements. The same year, FIC also stopped compiling statistics on technical cooperation with foreign companies. Prior to 1995, FIC reviewed such agreements and issued technical cooperation approvals to Taiwan companies that wished to licence foreign technology. Most of the approved agreements prior to 1995 were with Japanese companies. Of those agreements approved, most were in the electronics and electrical industries (30%) or the chemical industry (20%).

Trademark and service-mark licences must be registered with the Trademark Office of the National Bureau of Standards. In the mid-1990s, about 1,200–1,800 licences were approved each year.

Royalty percentages have been on the rise in Taiwan but are still below 5% of net sales. The exception is computer technology-related royalties, which have started to break the 10% royalty level. While royalties are usually based on net sales, some agreements have based them on production or output. Some foreign licensees have negotiated a base or minimum royalty level. Most licensing agreements run for five years.

The Business Infrastructure

Distribution

Taiwan's distribution system is notably complex. Despite some recent streamlining, it is likely to remain complex for the foreseeable future.

The distribution system is multi-staged, with up to two or three levels of wholesaling to service the small shops that still predominate in the Taiwan retail scene. It can be very frustrating for foreign businesses that try to deal directly with the distribution network here. Insider knowledge and connections are needed. The key to dealing with the system in Taiwan is a good agent.

A good agent will handle importation and set up a reliable marketing and distribution system for your product. With support from your firm, your agent in Taiwan can establish the right relationships for you as well as put together a workable network to get your product on the market. Adequate support means periodic visits to Taiwan by the exporter, a willingness to make product alterations to suit the market and an advertising campaign to push sales.

The Ports

Taiwan's Ministry of Transportation took over administration of the international harbours at Keelung, Taichung, Kaohsiung and Hualien in 1998. Under a plan adopted in 1997 to phase out the provincial government of Taiwan, these ports will be transferred from the provincial government to the national government's Ministry of Transportation and Communications (MOTC). MOTC is planning to upgrade its navigation and aviation department to a Bureau of Navigation Affairs before the year 2000. The new bureau will manage shipping and harbour affairs. Related jobs formerly administered by the provincial government, such as cargo loading, storage and warehousing, will be privatised.

Taiwan's largest port at Kaohsiung is the third busiest harbour in the world, after Hong Kong and Singapore.

Telecommunications

Taiwan was one of the last industrialised countries to liberalise its telecommunications market, which was significantly liberalised and opened to foreign investment on 1 July 1996. Prior to that, Taiwan's Directorate General of Telecommunications (DGT) was both a telecommunications regulatory agency and the sole provider of telecommunications services. For years, the DGT had enjoyed the enviable position of regulating itself.

As of 1 July 1996, the DGT was no longer the only buyer of telecommunications equipment like digital electronic switching equipment. This was significant to foreign equipment manufacturers because the DGT had limited its procurement list to just three joint venture sources—one with a German company and two with US firms.

With liberalisation, the telecommunications service supply function was taken from DGT and given to a new state-owned enterprise called Chunghwa Telecommunications Corporation

Direct ISDN telecommunications service between Singapore and Taiwan was inaugurated in 1995 as part of Taiwan's aggressive strategy to upgrade its telecommunications infrastructure.

(CHT). Telecommunications services have also been opened to private firms, which are no longer required to buy switching equipment from a restricted list of manufacturers approved by the DGT. Unfortunately, the state-owned CHT has been slow to respond to customer needs and hundreds of thousands of potential cellular customers were still waiting for service in early 1998. CHT has also been slow to provide interconnection arrangements to new market entrants and has continued to lease circuits at retail prices that are among the highest in the world.

For foreign investment purposes, telecommunications services were grouped into two categories. Category One services are open to foreign investment on a case-by-case basis and up to a maximum of 20% foreign ownership. Category Two services are not open to either new domestic investors or foreign private investors until the year 2001.

Category One services include services like mobile data, paging, trunked radio and mobile phones. These services have been opened to foreign investment, albeit on a limited basis, because foreign suppliers had some technological advantages that would help upgrade Taiwan's infrastructure. The authorities calculate that by limiting foreign investment to 20%, they will not jeopardise the nation's strategic security considerations.

Category Two services include the provision of local phone, long-distance phone and international phone. These services are very lucrative sectors where Taiwan already has a near-adequate infrastructure in place. The authorities would like to protect these profitable services for as long as possible.

The Financial System

Taiwan continues to liberalise its financial sector. It enacted a Futures Exchange law in 1997 and amended the Securities and Exchange Law in May 1997 to remove restrictions on employment of foreigners by securities firms. These laws will not, however, go into effect until Taiwan is admitted into WTO, where such laws are necessary for membership. By holding the enactment of these laws in abeyance, Taiwan is using them as a bargaining chip to gain admittance into WTO.

Limits remain on foreign ownership in listed companies. Foreign investors, both individuals and qualified foreign institutional investors, are subject to some limits on their portfolio investment as well as restrictions on their capital flows.

Banks

Taiwan's banking sector is divided into commercial banks, specialised banks, local branches of foreign banks and other banks established in accordance with laws other than the Banking Law. Commercial banks, specialised banks and local branches of foreign banks are allowed to undertake savings and trust business, as well as engage in securities operations. Before the establishment of 15 new private commercial banks in 1991, the banking sector was dominated by government-owned banks. The government's policy is to increase competition and further privatise the sector.

Investment and Trust Companies

Taiwan's investment and trust companies act as trustees to manage trust funds and trust properties by providing the customers with non-discretionary and discretionary account services. They also act as intermediaries to undertake investments with special purposes in the capital market. In recent years, the trend to reorganise investment and trust companies into commercial banks has been picking up steam.

The Postal Savings System

Although it only provides remitting and deposit taking services, the Postal Savings System, with over sixteen hundred postal offices throughout the island, account for the lion's share of total deposits accepted by all financial institutions in Taiwan. Deposits accepted by the Postal Savings System are still prohibited from being used to make loans immediately. Nevertheless, deposits accepted by the Postal Savings System may be freely re-deposited into banks or reinvested in various financial instruments.

Taiwan's Exchange Rate Policies

Taiwan has a floating exchange rate system in which banks set rates independently. The Taiwan government, however, controls the largest banks authorised to deal in foreign exchange. The Central Bank of China (CBC) intervenes in the foreign exchange market when it feels that speculation or "drastic fluctuations" in the exchange rate may impair normal market adjustments. CBC uses direct foreign exchange trading by its surrogate banks and public policy statements as the main tools to influence exchange rates. Since July 1996, CBC has ceased to set banks' overbought and oversold positions. Banks are now authorised to set these positions. In May 1997, CBC lifted limits on banks' foreign liabilities. CBC, however, still limits the use of derivative products denominated in New Taiwan dollars.

Trade-related funds flow freely in and out of Taiwan. Most restrictions on capital account flows have been removed since late 1995. Laws restricting repatriation of the principal and earnings from direct investment have been lifted in principle, but some necessary amendments are still pending in the legislative yuan. Despite significant easing of previous restrictions on foreign portfolio investment, some limits remain.

Financial Disclosure for Public Corporations
In the United States and most other developed nations, the profits of publicly-traded companies are known within days of a quarter's end. In Taiwan, however, public companies are not required to release results until 30 days after the end of a quarter and full financial statements are required for 90 days. As a result, the stocks of Taiwan companies can rise as profits are tumbling—or vice versa.

Electronic Commerce Coming of Age in Taiwan
The electronic commerce industry in Taiwan is growing at an incredible rate of 10% per month. The Internet Shopping market in Taiwan is expected to increase from estimated revenues of NT$3 billion in 1997 to NT$20 billion by the year 2000. The increasing popularity of the Internet, coupled with the Taiwan authorities' desire to transform Taiwan into an "intelligent island", has led to significant government budgets for information infrastructure programmes. Taiwan has invested in fibre-optic networks and computer training for students. Visitors to Kaohsiung's City Hall can access the city's services through computer terminals in the lobby.

As of 1997, there were approximately 700,000 Internet users in Taiwan. The government projects that the number of Internet users will reach 3 million by the year 2000. By 1998, over 1,000 web sites had been established and it is estimated that there would be 3,000 sites by the year 2000. According to the Market Intelligence Centre (MIC) of the Information Industry Institute of Taiwan, the primary Internet users in Taiwan are single (74%) and most of them are males (75%). The education level of Internet users is college level or higher (83%), while the average age is between 16 and 35 years (89%). The average access time is 7.84 hours, with 66% of users accessing the Internet from homes and 18% accessing it from offices. Among these users, 42% browsed virtual shops, but only 12% of this actually shop in it (domestic and overseas included). The consumption value of each Internet purchase ranges from NT$1,000 to NT$2,000. Payment methods are via credit cards, bank wire transfer, postal remittance, fax credit information and cash on delivery (COD).

Publications, computers and computer peripherals are the most frequently purchased items at present. For the future, video tapes/CDs and various programme and airline tickets are predicted to become the most popular items purchased. However, problems still abound because the technical aspects of on-line commerce in Taiwan are still not very sophisticated.

Labour

Taiwan's labour unions are company-specific, as in Japan, rather than industry-wide, as they are in Europe and the United States. A company labour union can be formed with as few as 30 employee members. Taiwan's unions have historically been moderate in demands and strikes have been rare. Labour union membership has been dropping since the late 1980s.

Taiwanese employees enjoy 18 national holidays a year. Most Taiwanese work a five and a half day work week and get off at noon on Saturdays. Most foreign corporations in Taiwan follow a five-day work week. Vacation time averages 10–12 days a year after the first year of employment.

Under Taiwan's Labour Union Law, the right of association of workers is still restricted. The law not only forbids civil servants, teachers and defence industry workers from organising trade unions, it also forbids workers from forming competing trade unions and confederations. However, through the process of democratisation, workers have gradually established a number of independent labour organisations either legally or illegally.

Union membership fell during the 1995–1998 period due in large part to an increase in the number of foreign guest workers and a slowdown in the rate of economic growth and new job growth. Foreign guest workers, primarily from the Philippines, are allowed into Taiwan for a couple of years to work in low-wage assembly-line positions. The transitory nature of their work does not lend itself to union membership.

With the exception of civil servants, teachers and defence industry workers, the Labour Union Law, the Law Governing the Handling of Labour Disputes and the Collective Agreement Law give workers the right to organise and bargain collectively. However, the laws restrict workers' ability to exercise these rights. The Labour Union Law, for example, stipulates that workers shall not strike to demand an increase in wages exceeding standard wages. Collective bargaining agreements exist mainly in large-scale enterprises.

The Labour Standards Law stipulates the minimum age of employment to be 15, after completion of a nine-year compulsory education. County and city labour bureaus enforce minimum age laws. Child labour is rare in Taiwan. The Labour Standards Law also mandates labour standards. As of 1997, the law covered 3.4 million of Taiwan's 6.3 million salaried workers. The law limits the work-week to 48 hours (eight hours per day, six days per week) and requires that workers get a day off every seven days.

In addition to wages, employers typically provide workers with additional payments and benefits, including national health insurance and labour insurance premiums, labour welfare funds and meal and transportation allowances. Taiwan's working conditions have been improved significantly with increasing economic growth. In terms of wages and other benefits, the rights of workers do not vary significantly by industrial sector.

A Management Shortage

Taiwan's manufacturers are scrambling to find talented people to man their operations. Operational skills are wanting at many of the island's rapidly-expanding companies. Many companies have not invested in the ongoing professional development of their management. This is especially true in the information technology sector. Even if you emptied East and Southeast Asia of engineers, you would have a hard time staffing all the computer-related plants that are being established in Taiwan.

Look under the "hood" of Taiwan's largest corporations, especially those that are family-owned, and management is often a mess. The companies have the drive and entrepreneurial spirit, but they have not invested enough in the management systems required to keep pace with growth. Taiwan is strong in engineering and management talent but lacking in trained individuals.

The management skills gap is worst in Taiwan's multinational corporations. Companies such as Acer Incorporated, Taiwan's US$6 billion computer and IT industry giant, can attract the skilled Taiwan talent needed to run their operations at home but not in their overseas plants. Acer, with over 30 overseas plants, has had to give more and more autonomy over to local management in its overseas plants because headquarters does not yet have the management depth to operate globally.

Retail Trends

Taiwan's retail scene is changing dramatically. Although "traditional" stores, or small to medium-sized family-owned stores, still contribute the largest proportion of retail sales, "modern" retail store sales are expanding more rapidly. Hypermarkets, warehouse

Old-style department stores are battling with Taiwan's new shopping malls for young consumers. Many are expanding into newer suburbs to reach new customers.

stores, supermarkets, convenience stores and shopping malls are claiming retail ground formerly occupied by the older department stores and "mum and pop" stores. Sales in the modern retail outlets grew by a remarkable 23% in 1995 and is expected to continue growing rapidly because of trends in consumption patterns, where young consumers prefer to shop at "modern" retail stores. It is estimated that the total sales generated by these modern retail stores will reach US$26 billion in the year 2000, more than triple the 1995 level of US$8.4 billion "Traditional" stores sales growth is expected to expand by slightly over 90% over the same period, to US$196 billion.

Savvy retailers are heeding these forecasts and are rapidly expanding their operations by opening new outlets and branch stores. About 600 convenience stores open in Taiwan annually; warehouse stores, on their part, try to acquire more land for expansion. In addition, domestic companies are investing in shopping mall projects for large-scale retail operations and more than 20 shopping mall projects have been approved by MOEA. The construction of these shopping malls is expected to be completed by 2000.

Convenience Stores

From a street corner on Chungshan North Road in Taipei, it is possible to see three 7-11 convenience stores. In 1995, there were 3,200 convenience stores in Taiwan—one for every 10,000 people. There will soon be one store for every 4,000 people. The convenience store boom began in 1980 with the opening of the first Western-style convenience store chain. Over one-third (1,150) of all convenience stores in Taiwan are 7-11s. The rest include President (650), Family Mart (280), Hi-Life (230) and OK (210).

Department Stores

The three largest department store chains in Taiwan—Far Eastern, Sogo Pacific and Shin-Kong Mitsukoshi—are expanding their store locations dramatically. Most of the expansion sites are in satellite cities ringing Taipei, Taichung and Kaohsiung. Far Eastern Department Stores undertook a dramatic expansion programme in 1996, with the aim to expand from 11 to 15 stores by the year 2000. In 1998, there were 23 large department stores in Taipei, six in the Taoyuan/Hsinchu area, seven in Taichung and five in Kaohsiung. In 1997, these large department stores totalled sales of approximately US$3.4 billion, a 15% increase over 1996.

Supermarkets

Supermarkets are expanding rapidly as well. The largest supermarket chain, Wellcome, plans to expand from 100 stores in 1996 to 200 stores by the end of the century. Most of the expansions are expected to be in southern Taiwan. In 1996, there were over 1,000 supermarkets on the island.

Warehouse Stores

Carrefour, the largest warehouse store in Taiwan, had 11 branches in 1996. Carrefour began by leasing store space but is now building its own stores. Costco, a joint venture of Taiwan's President Department Store Group and US Pricecostco, plans to open 10–12 stores in Taiwan by the year 2000. Makro, the Dutch warehouse club operator, had managed US$1 billion in annual sales with only seven stores in 1994.

Foreign retailers who can compete with a low-price strategy, unique products or innovative merchandising can find opportunities in Taiwan. Consumers in Taiwan are starting to shop at high-end retail stores, which offer distinctive goods and services as well as at large-scale stores, which offer a wide variety of competitively priced goods.

Shopping Malls

Large American-style suburban shopping malls began appearing in Taiwan in the late 1990s after the government created tax incentives for them. In fact, 21 shopping mall projects, with a total capital investment of over US$5.0 billion, have obtained approval from MOEA.

Lucky Eights and Off Numbers: Superstitions in Business

Most Chinese are extremely superstitious and the Taiwanese are no exception. When faced with an important decision, the Chinese always look for an auspicious sign. Ever since the ancient Shang Dynasty when they used cracked tortoise shells and animal shoulder blades to predict the future, the Chinese have searched for omens to foretell their futures. When setting a wedding date, opening a new business or breaking ground for a new building, the Taiwanese will select auspicious dates on which to hold these events and use auspicious colours and symbols in these events.

The Inauspicious Seventh Lunar Month

Some Taiwanese Buddhists believe that the ghosts of heaven and hell return to Earth during the seventh lunar month. If your business partner subscribes to this belief, he or she may want to delay negotiations and decisions until the inauspicious month has passed. The seventh lunar month normally coincides with or overlaps part of the Gregorian calendar's August. While it is wise to not ask others about their religious beliefs, it is helpful to be aware that such beliefs may be behind perplexing delays in doing business.

Much of the superstition surrounding numbers comes from the Chinese belief that similar sounds produce similar results. Thus, the number four is unlucky because the Mandarin pronunciations of "four" and "death" are similar. The Chinese preoccupation with fate and luck has spawned so many superstitious beliefs—many of them contradictory—that it can be overwhelming not only to foreigners but to the Chinese themselves. For the Chinese, it's possible to find an auspicious aspect to virtually any situation.

Odd Numbers Out

The Chinese character for "odd" (as in "odd numbers") also means "alone". The Chinese dislike for aloneness carries over into their superstitions regarding numbers. They prefer things to come in pairs, even numbers. Good fortune comes in pairs. Gifts, for example, should be given in even numbers if possible. Dishware, cups and cash should only be given in even numbers. However, this does not mean you have to give a pair of ties, two bread toasters and other items that are normally given in singles.

Deadly Fours

Watch out for "fours". Since the Chinese word for "four" (*si*) is pronounced like the Chinese word for "death", the numeral four is considered unlucky in some situations. Most buildings in Taiwan do not have a level designated as the "fourth floor". They skip from three to five when labelling their floors. Residents on the fourth floors of high-rise apartment buildings often pay less for their apartments than do residents on more "auspicious" floors.

Airlines flying to and from Taiwan also report that flights on the fourth of each month are more lightly booked than on other dates. Many Chinese think it is unlucky to travel on the fourth. If you are flying in the first week of the month and have difficulty getting a seat (not uncommon in this highly regulated market), ask the reservation agent to look for something on the fourth. Chances are, you will get the seat you want.

Lucky Sixes and Eights

The Chinese consider the numbers six and eight lucky numbers. The origin of the former's auspiciousness is not certain. Some explain that the number six is lucky because it is the highest number on the dice. Others explain that it is considered lucky because its pronunciation in Hokkien sounds like the English word "luck". The number eight is considered auspicious because in Cantonese, "eight" and "success" are pronounced similarly. Most Chinese will go to great lengths to associate themselves with "sixes" and "eights".

Recently, Taiwanese bureaucrats decided to auction off auto licence plates with auspicious numbers. This has proven to be a financial boon to the government. In the early 1990s, Taiwan's Jihsheng Securities Company spent NT$600,000 to buy the licence plate with the number "8888". High prices are paid for any combination of "sixes" and "eights".

Lucky Addresses

Chinese businesses and families also open businesses or buy residences that have lucky addresses. One savvy American real estate agent in Oklahoma searches her database of available houses for street addresses with "sixes" and "eights" whenever she has a Chinese client. Houses at "888 Northwest 8th Street" or "66 North

Stiles" are premium addresses to most Chinese. They certainly are providential for sellers wise enough to seek out Chinese buyers willing to pay a premium for lucky addresses.

Addresses extend even to hotel room numbers. Travelling Taiwan business people like to stay in rooms 168, 518, 688, 816 or 888. Some hotels in Macau, the PRC and Taiwan even charge a higher rate for rooms with lucky numbers. If you are entertaining Taiwan business partners in your hometown, you can make a good impression or at least enhance their feeling of "rightness" about the deal under discussion by reserving rooms with these numbers for them.

Lucky Prices

You may notice that in some small Taiwanese retail stores, there is a preponderance of price tags featuring lucky numbers. Some business people feel that auspicious prices on their goods help sell them. Indeed, superstitious customers sometimes do make goods thus priced the best sellers. The number "168" is a homophone for "the road to success" and, thus, prices from NT$168 to NT$168,000 (and beyond) are favourable prices.

Feng Shui for Business

The Chinese desire for harmony extends to nature and the spiritual relationship between physical things like hills, valleys, water and man-made structures. The Chinese belief in the propitiousness of the proper placement of man-made structures within nature began with efforts to locate good burial sites for their dead. To ensure that their deceased family members would enjoy harmony with nature, the Chinese employed several guidelines to select the sites. Eventually, the guidelines was applied to all buildings and structures.

These guidelines developed into the science of geomancy or *feng shui*, which literally means "wind and water", two of the basic elements of nature. A cadre of professional geomancers arose to help the uninitiated understand the guidelines and design their structures in ways that would ensure success and protect the health and well-being of those who used the structures. Today, feng shui experts from Taipei to Vancouver are consulted by architects and builders before construction starts. New office tenants hire geomancers to assist with remodelling and layout.

The central responsibility of the geomancer is to arrange structure, furniture, doors, etc. in a way to let the *qi* or the "cosmic breath of the dragon" flow unimpeded. There is "good qi" and "bad qi". The geomancer tries to arrange doors and other openings in ways that let good qi in and keep bad qi out. The result is usually an aesthetically pleasing organisation of space.

Feng shui consultants will ultimately recommend that you change the way you arrange things. If you fail to implement the recommended changes, any downturns in business will be blamed on your unwillingness to heed the advice of the consultant. Building owner-tenants will hardly ever find a feng shui consultant who recommends that they keep everything as they were before.

For a detailed discussion of how feng shui relates to business, do read *Feng Shui for Business* by Evelyn Lip (Times Books International, Singapore).

Chapter 5

Investing In or Setting Up a Business in Taiwan

It may come as a surprise, but business people with cross-straits* experience say that it is more difficult to set up a foreign-owned business in Taiwan than in the People's Republic of China. Undoubtedly this is true in varying degrees, depending on what type of business is involved. Taiwan's authorities no longer welcome low-wage, labour-intensive manufacturing industries. Neither do the people welcome "dirty" industries like chemical manufacturing. Heavy manufacturing is being driven from Taiwan to the PRC or Southeast Asia by environmental, space, and economic pressures in the former. High-tech "clean" industries, such as information technology, biomedical, aerospace and some service industries, are, however, welcomed.

In 1996, Taiwan eased restrictions on foreign investment. The telecommunications and real estate industries were opened to foreign investors, subject to ownership limits and approval requirements. The country lifted all restrictions on investments by foreigners in petroleum refining, coal coking and in the production of digital switching office systems. It has also removed many other barriers to foreign investment, abolishing export performance and local content requirements (except in the automobile and motorcycle industries), and liberalising repatriation of their earning and capital remittances. Investments in electricity generation has been open to foreigners since 1994.

Foreign ownership limits for insurance, securities, banks, offshore futures brokering, foreign exchange brokerage and

---

* "Cross-straits" refers to the Taiwan Strait that separates the island of Taiwan from mainland China. The term is commonly used to refer to matters involving both Taiwan and the PRC.

securities investment trust companies have been removed since 1996. Foreign ownership limits for shipping companies and foreign forwarders were raised from one-third to half in late 1996. Other industries with foreign ownership limits include real estate leasing (90%), mining (50%), trust companies (40%), cement (50 %) and air transport (33%)

Ask Yourself Some Key Questions

Reliable information about the Taiwanese market is not difficult to get if you can read Chinese or can pay someone to get the information for you. Both domestic and international market research firms are well established in Taiwan and many government trade agencies supply free or low-cost market data and analysis to their home-country businesses. Whether you use these sources or not, you need to ask yourself some key questions:

- Is my product/service already on the market in Taiwan?
- Is my product/service allowed to be traded in Taiwan?
- Are there trade barriers or political factors that will keep me out of the market?
- Have my competitors already carved a niche for themselves? Are domestic competitors protected from foreign competition?
- What is it going to take in capital, human resources and patience to crack this market?
- How will I distribute my product?
- What sales strategy should I adopt?
- What are my short-term, medium-term and long-term goals in the Taiwanese market?

Many of these questions can be answered, at least partially, before your first visit to Taiwan.

Types of Business Enterprises Allowed

Foreign companies are allowed to establish several types of business enterprises in Taiwan. They include the following: companies, partnerships, branches, representative offices, liaison offices or job-site offices. Before deciding on the type of business enterprise, you should seek the counsel of a Taiwan-based legal and/or accounting firm.

It is advantageous for a foreign investor to file as a "Foreign Investment Approval" (FIA) company. An FIA company is one that has been approved by the Investment Commission of MOEA under the Statute for the Investment by Foreign Nationals. A non-FIA company, although owned by foreigners, is set up according to the Company Law and not the Statute for Investment by Foreign Nationals. With a non-FIA company, the investment must be made in New Taiwan dollars. It is subject to restrictions regarding local residence, nationality and the investment amount stipulated in the ROC Company Law.

Company Types

The four types of companies that can be established by foreigners in Taiwan are:

- **Limited company**: A company formed by five to 21 shareholders, where each shareholder's liability is limited to the amount of contributed capital.

- **Unlimited company**: A company formed by two or more shareholders that bear unlimited joint liability for the obligations of the company.

- **Company limited by shares**: A public or private company formed by seven or more shareholders, where the total capital of the company is divided into shares and each shareholder is liable up to the amount of contributed capital.

- **Unlimited company with limited liability shareholders**: A company formed by one or more shareholders of limited liability. The unlimited liability shareholders bear unlimited joint liability for the obligations of the company. The limited liability shareholders' liabilities are limited to the amount of contributed capital.

Branch
While a subsidiary in Taiwan is considered an independent juridical person, a branch is considered to be part of its parent company. A branch is not allowed to undertake manufacturing without approval. Company Law requires a branch to obtain approval from MOEA. Branches must meet minimum capital requirements.

Representative Office
Foreign companies can set up a representative office in Taiwan to carry out legal matters in the country and to act as an agent of the parent company. A representative office cannot conduct profit-seeking business. Negotiating and concluding contracts, and sourcing products are legitimate activities of a representative office.

Liaison Office
Liaison offices have similar functions to representative offices but can also engage in market research, public relations and communications. Registration with MOEA is not required but without registration, local bank accounts cannot be obtained.

Partnership
Individuals, including foreigners, can set up a general partnership in Taiwan. Partners are legally and financially responsible for (court) judgements made against their company. There is no cap on their financial exposure.

Sole Proprietorship

Foreigners are also allowed to establish a sole proprietorship in Taiwan. Here too the owner bears unlimited liabilities.

Joint Venture

Joint ventures are not juridical entities in Taiwan. A joint venture is not recognised by the court as a legal entity that can be sued. Only the corporations that comprise the joint venture can be sued, or otherwise be subject to legal action.

Application Procedures

Registration

This is where it gets complicated. It is definitely an area where you will need the help of a Taiwan-based attorney experienced in registering foreign companies. The procedures vary according to the type of business enterprise you wish to set up.

Foreigners who wish to set up a manufacturing facility in Taiwan should contact MOEA's Industrial Development and Investment Centre (IDIC) in Taipei.

Foreigners must apply for permission to invest in Taiwan (forms are available from IDIC). MOEA will review the application, which generally takes three to five weeks to complete.

Labour

Finding Employees

The availability of labour varies according to industry and function. There continues to be a shortage of labour in what the Taiwanese call the "3-D industries"—dirty, dangerous and demanding—such as construction, assembly lines and heavy machinery repair work. Companies affected have had to import willing and less expensive "guest workers" on short or medium-term contracts from Southeast Asia to fill positions in factories. The use of guest workers is strictly controlled and no company can have more than 35% of its workforce made up of guest workers.

New recruits are usually attracted through newspaper advertisements, executive search firms and personnel agencies. Taiwan's Council of Labour Affairs helps employers find potential workers. There are no government controls on the hiring process of local workers. Foreign companies are free to interview and hire whoever they wish.

Many temporary staffing agencies in Taiwan can supply foreign businesses with clerical, administrative or technical personnel on a short-term basis. The shortage of computer programmers and other technicians has resulted in many foreign manufacturers filling positions in these fields with temporary staff.

Company loyalty is almost nonexistent in Taiwan. The turnover rates are as high as 30% among junior staff due to labour shortage and the Taiwanese penchant for wanting to strike out on one's own to form one's own business. One way to combat the high turnover is to have current employees recommend their friends and classmates to the company. This creates some obligation on the new recruit to not cause his/her friend to lose face by quitting too soon. However, mass resignation of friends who want to start a new business does occasionally occur.

Returning Taiwanese

There is a shortage of engineers and technical personnel in Taiwan. The Taiwanese government and companies have tapped into the large numbers of overseas Taiwanese to try and fill these positions. Many Taiwanese leave the country to attend universities in the United States and Europe. Taiwan has been very successful in recruiting these bilingual expatriate Taiwanese for high-paying technical jobs.

The ROC government actively recruits overseas Taiwanese who have completed their university training and worked in technical jobs abroad. The government has set up a web page (in

Chinese) on the Internet to inform overseas Taiwanese of the incentives they would receive if they returned to Taiwan with their experience and skills. These returnees are often offered employment packages more lucrative than those offered to local recruits. The returnees also tend to rise through the corporate hierarchy much more quickly than local recruits—thus creating tension between the returning expatriates and those who had stayed in Taiwan for their education.

Wages and Bonuses

In 1995, the average wage for locally hired typists with a high school diploma was NT$18,000 per month plus almost two months bonus at the end of the year. Executive secretaries with a college degree get an average of NT$45,000 per month.

It is customary for employers in Taiwan to give their workers a year end bonus equal to one to three months' pay. The competition for workers has become so intense that companies have developed new recruitment packages that include club memberships, profit sharing schemes and low interest loans.

Land and Industrial Parks

Obtaining Land

After obtaining approval from the Investment Commission to set up a company in Taiwan, the company can purchase or lease lands for business operation. The government has established over 80 industrial zones and export-processing zones where land is available for approved investors. For help in obtaining land, contact the Industrial Development Bureau of MOEA.

Taxation and Profit Remittance

Taxation

MOF administers the tax laws in Taiwan. Most foreign corporations pay a corporation tax rate of 22% or 25%. A 20% withholding tax is imposed on interest, dividends, fees and royalties. The value-added tax (VAT) is 5%. Progressive personal tax rates range from 6% to 40%.

Foreign companies and individuals are liable for individual income taxes and corporate income tax only on income generated in Taiwan.

Taxes	
Company Tax	The maximum tax rate on business income is set at 25%.
Personal Income Tax	The upper limit for consolidated (personal) income is 40%.
Value-Added Tax	A 5% flat-rate tariff applies.
Tariff	The average nominal tariff rate for imported goods is 8.89%. Out of this figure, the rate for industrial products is 6.52% and that for agricultural products 21.63%.
Harbour Construction Fee	Exported and imported products are subject to a harbour construction fee that is equal to 0.5% of the assessed value.

Business Taxes

There are two basic types of business taxes in Taiwan—the Gross Business Receipts Tax (GBRT) and the Value Added Tax (VAT). The GBRT is levied on traders dealing in agricultural commodities as well as on financial institutions, certain food and beverage companies, and other businesses that MOF has exempted from reporting sales transactions. The 5% VAT is paid on the value added at each stage of a transaction.

Profit Remittances

Foreign investors are able to remit profits made in Taiwan back to their home country. The procedure to do so requires that the investor apply to remit either the yearly income or the net profit of the Taiwan-based investment. After one year of operation, investors can also apply to remit the entire amount of their investment principal. This also applies to capital gains realised from the investment.

Residence and Visas

Visas for Investors and Workers

Companies or organisations in Taiwan must apply to the ROC government for permission to employ foreign nationals. A foreigner cannot work legally in Taiwan without such a permit. There are two kinds of visas for foreigners investing in Taiwan: visitor visas and resident visas. Visitor visas are applicable to foreign nationals planning to stay in Taiwan for less than six months for transit, tour, visit, study or business. Resident visas are needed by foreign nationals planning to stay in Taiwan for more than six months to live with relatives, attend school, invest or work.

Approved foreign investors who wish to employ foreign specialists, technicians and administrative personnel must apply to the Investment Commission of MOEA for approval. Upon approval, the investor can apply for the employees' entry visa from the Ministry of Foreign Affairs.

Living in Taiwan

Expatriates and their families moving to Taiwan can get help from the non-profit Community Service Centre in Taipei. The centre publishes *Taipei Living*, a book that gives tips on living in Taipei and applicable to other Taiwanese cities as well. The centre also offers newcomers orientation services and school referrals.

Investment Incentives

As part of the ROC government's Asia-Pacific Regional Operations Centre (APROC) strategy (see p. 29 of chapter 1), the government set up the "APROC Window", a special one-stop centre for foreign investors. The APROC Window can assist qualifying investors through the bureaucracy.

Details about Taiwan's investment incentives are available from the IDIC of MOEA.

Day-to-Day Hassles

Setting Up a Bank Account

It is not easy to establish a business bank account in Taiwan. MOEA must issue an approval letter before the bank can open a demand deposit account or cheque account. The entire process for setting up a business account can take three to six months. In addition to the MOEA approval letter, the following documents may be required by the bank:

- Power of Attorney establishing the person in charge and giving authorised signatures
- ID or passport of the person
- Certified copies of the business registration documents
- Letter of Introduction

117

All inward and outward remittances of foreign currencies or those involving conversion between New Taiwan dollars and foreign currencies are reported to the Central Bank of China.

There are many commercial and retail banks in Taiwan. Many of these have island-wide branches and even overseas branches. Since 1992, a number of medium-sized entrepreneurial banks with 10–30 branches have been established to fill the gaps in services not offered by the more established, larger banks. These new banks are more flexible and are in many ways more competitive than the "old-style" banks.

Foreign Exchange Controls

After four decades of severe limitations on foreign currency holdings and outflows, Taiwan relaxed foreign exchange controls in 1987. Since 1993, the central bank has raised the ceiling for inward and outward remittances converted into or out of New Taiwan dollars. There are no limits on inward or outward remittances not converted into or out of New Taiwan dollars.

Temporary Office Space

In the major cities, there are temporary office agencies that provide ready-to-use office space—with telephones, fax machines, a mail drop and a secretary—for companies in the process of setting up operations in Taiwan. By using these temporary offices, foreign companies can bypass the hassle of obtaining fax, telephone, clerical (administrative equipment and services) and mailing services on short notice. This allows the new entrant to the Taiwan market to focus on getting his/her business off the ground in the first crucial weeks or months.

Leasing an Office

It is generally a renter's market in Taiwan's office leasing world. Rent normally has to be paid in advance every month or quarter. In the 1990s, annual rent increases averaged 5%–7%. When

Office space is adequate but expensive in Taiwan's business centres. Temporary offices with office equipment and secretarial services are widely available.

sourcing for offices, be sure to inquire about management fees, security deposits and other costs that are not part of the quoted monthly rent. Utilities and maintenance costs are not usually revealed by landlords unless specifically asked for. Remember that a value-added tax of 5% of the rent is payable to the government.

Space is usually given in *ping* rather than square metres or feet. One ping is the equivalent of 3.3 sq. m. Note that most landlords include common areas such as lobbies, toilets and stairways in their space quotation. To derive the actual usable space, subtract the common areas from the gross quotation.

Most landlords require leases of two to three years in duration, with substantial penalty clauses for early termination. If you need to exit an agreement early, let the landlord know as soon as possible. A penalty fee of three to six months is common. A refundable security deposit (without interest) of approximately three to six months' rent is standard.

Chapter 6

Selling to Taiwan

Learn from the Japanese Approach

The Japanese have been very successful doing business in Taiwan. Unlike other countries, they have a cultural and historical relationship with Taiwan from which important lessons can be learnt. Japanese companies are so firmly entrenched in Taiwan that they are hardly even visible as being distinctively Japanese. The keys to Japanese success in Taiwan are their:

- Long-term view
- Top to bottom network of relationships

From the beginning, Japanese companies were in Taiwan for the long haul. They send their executives to language schools to learn not just Mandarin but also Taiwanese, the language of the locals, business people and customers. The Japanese also keep a low profile in Taiwan that allows them to avoid controversy. Many Japanese companies will clinch a deal first and worry about making money later.

Japanese companies also work to build networks from the top to the bottom of Taiwan's governmental and business systems. When it comes to winning major projects, most foreigners tend to focus on the ROC central government. The Japanese, on the other hand, network with everyone, from county officials to consultants, suppliers and academics, as well as the provincial and central government officials. With contacts at all levels, the Japanese can easily outflank the competition.

A comparison of the differences between the Japanese and Western approaches to business dealings in Taiwan is summarised on the following page:

The Japanese Approach versus the Western Approach

Japanese Approach	Western Approach
Begin by establishing personal relationships to determine the other side's strengths and weaknesses	Arrive with lawyers for first round of negotiations
Establish contacts at all levels of government (central, provincial, city)	Focus on establishing contacts at the highest levels of the central government
Show maximum flexibility towards the other side's processes	Show preference for familiar processes and well-laid plans
Work to establish a high degree of trust	Keep the other party at arm's length
Maintain constant contact with Taiwanese partners	Make infrequent visits to Taiwan; maintain limited personal contact with Taiwanese partners
Sort problems out as they occur	Plan financial returns well
Keep a low profile and avoid publicity	Get maximum press coverage when deals are clinched
No clear lines between business and pleasure	Separate business and pleasure as much as possible
Learn both Chinese and Taiwanese	Make little effort to learn or use the Chinese language

Source: Australian Business Centre, Taipei

First Things First—Market Research

Do not do anything in Taiwan until you have done your research. Too many foreign companies have hooked up with the wrong Taiwanese partner or squandered money trying to sell their product the same way that they did at home. Many have the mistaken notion that the Taiwanese market will respond the same way as their home market. Just because your product sells well at home is no guarantee that it will sell well in Taiwan.

The way to avoid expensive mistakes is to do your research beforehand. There are several sources of market research information to consider:

- Market research divisions of advertising agencies
- Media consulting firms
- Banks and investment institutions that survey specific businesses
- Marketing research firms
- Freelance researchers
- Universities and research institutions
- Government agencies

There are 25 to 30 market research companies and specialists in Taiwan. The most comprehensive listing of these firms can be found on the Internet (see appendix D for the relevant addresses). Their research methodologies and capabilities, however, vary widely. Most market research companies specialise along industry, geographic or methodological lines. For example, some specialise in research on the electronics industry, while others specialise in market research in Taipei only or in a certain methodology, such as consumer surveys. Before deciding on a research company to employ, conduct your own survey and find out which company best suits your needs.

Most foreign companies tend to use subsidiaries of well-known international market research agencies, such as the Survey Research Group.

Another good (and often free) source of industry-specific information are the hundreds of trade associations in Taiwan. Almost every industry and business sector in Taiwan has its own trade association. Everyone from the exporters of plastic Christmas trees to shipbuilders has their own association. Many of these trade associations handle trade and investment inquiries. Many also have English publications about their industry. A list of trade associations is included in appendix B of this book.

The commercial development offices of foreign embassies and trade offices also undertake market research that is available to companies from their home country. The American Institute in Taiwan (AIT), for example, commissions research on topics of interest to US exporters. Most of the research sponsored by foreign governments is let out to local subcontractors. Off-the-shelf research reports are generally available free-of-charge to companies from the sponsoring country.

Customised, project-specific market research can also be commissioned by many of the foreign embassies and trade offices in Taiwan. The US Department of Commerce (USDOC), for example, will conduct customised research for a US client willing to pay around US$2,500 for the work. Most of the customised research commissioned by entities like the USDOC is done by subcontractors. USDOC adds its commission on top of the fee of the subcontractor. Your advantage in going through your government trade agency to get the research by the third party research firm is the increased likelihood that the product will be monitored for quality by your government's representatives.

The governments of Taiwan, the United States, Japan, Korea, Australia, the United Kingdom, Canada and Singapore have market research available on-line or via CD-ROM.

Taiwan society is changing so quickly that consumer research can be outdated in just six months. Marketers must bear in mind that consumers here, like those elsewhere, are fickle.

Other Providers of Market Information:

The Board of Foreign Trade (BOFT)
The ROC government's Board of Foreign Trade (BOFT) should be one of your first stops for basic market data. An agency of MOEA, BOFT collects and disseminates information on imports and exports. Using BOFT data, you can determine how much of a product is imported and the countries it is imported from. You can also determine the companies importing certain foods and what percentage of the imports are attributable to each importer.

A nut exporter, for example, could use BOFT data to determine that 98% of all almonds imported into Taiwan come from the United States. The exporter could also determine that there are 74 importers of nuts in Taiwan and that three (Lian Hwa Foods, Hai Jyi Foods and Uming Company) account for about 70% of all imported nuts to Taiwan. Much of the data is already analysed by the various national export development agencies (such as the US Department of Agriculture's Foreign Agricultural Service) and can be obtained from these agencies.

ROC National Central Library (NCL)
The Reader Services Division of the National Central Library (NCL) maintains on-line directories of Taiwan government publications, which are accessible via the Internet. One of the most interesting aspects of the NCL site is the section entitled "Reports on Overseas Assignments by Agency Officials of the Executive Yuan". Professionals sent overseas by the ROC government must submit reports upon their return to Taiwan. Since 1970, the NCL has compiled all reports onto a CD-ROM. These reports are valuable information for businesses engaged in researching the strategies of competitors. The CD-ROM is only available in Chinese.

Designed to announce information on government publications, the on-line directory includes bibliographic citations of public documents generated by the ROC government since 1984. The documents include books, journals and non-printed materials, and cover a wide range of topics like statistics, political science, social science, economics, science and technology, education, finance, law, literature, art and religion.

Advertising and the Media

Taiwan is the third largest advertising market in Asia. Only Japan and Korea have larger total advertising expenditures. In 1995, total advertising expenditures in Taiwan surpassed the US$3.5 billion mark and is growing at the rate of about 10% a year. Rising wages and an increase in purchasing power, coupled with the opening of the market to foreign competition, have driven the boom in advertising. The liberalisation of the media has also contributed to the rise of advertising in the country. There are more newspapers, radio stations and cable TV networks to carry advertising than before.

The inroads into the market made by foreign-based multinationals in recent years have forced Taiwan's home-grown firms to promote their brands more aggressively. Taiwan's advertising industry has benefited from the intense competition for the consumer's brand loyalty. And consumers have more to spend than ever. Average monthly household disposable income in Taiwan in 1995 exceeded US$31,500, a 27% increase over 1991.

Foreign brands are enjoying increasing popularity with Taiwan's cash-rich consumers. Imported high-quality products are often preferred over domestic brands. In 1995, imports of foreign-made consumers goods into the country were valued at over US$12 billion, almost double the 1991 level of US$6.8 billion.

Advertising Agencies

Many of Taiwan's 180 domestic and 22 foreign registered advertising agencies offer market research, concept, design and media placement services. A directory of Taiwan's advertising agencies and their specialities is available on the Internet.

If you use a multinational advertising agency to handle your advertising campaign in Taiwan, make sure the agency assigns an account manager that fully understands the Taiwanese market and your business culture. Agencies have also had difficulties recruiting qualified staff to handle international accounts. The standard of English among Taiwanese advertising personnel is not as high as that in Singapore, Hong Kong or Malaysia.

The Media

A 1997 survey conducted by the Directorate-General of Budget, Accounting and Statistics (DGBAS) of the executive yuan revealed that the major indoor recreational activity of the Taiwanese was watching television or videos. People spent an average of 2.25 hours daily watching televisions or videos, 25 minutes reading newspapers or magazines and 15 minutes listening to music. Men spent more time reading newspapers or magazines, while women preferred watching television, videos or listening to music. The two groups that spent the most time watching television or videos were those in the age groups, 50–64 years and 15–24 years. The amount of time spent watching television was considerably higher among those with less education.

Free-to-air television and newspapers are the most popular means of advertising in Taiwan, with approximately 80% of all advertising expenditures spent on these two media. In 1997, local advertisers spent over US$1 billion on the three free-to-air television networks. Advertising expenditures for magazines and radio broadcasting are not significant in Taiwan. Each accounts for only about 5% of total advertising expenditure.

Television Television advertising is growing rapidly, but at 35% of all advertising spending in Taiwan, television as an advertising medium still lags considerably behind the West (over 50%) and

Japan (45%). There are three national television networks in Taiwan: China Television Company (CTV), Taiwan Television Enterprise (TTV) and China Television Service (CTS). All three networks are regulated by the Government Information Office (GIO), which controls the amount of advertising time on television.

Programming is primarily in Chinese. Subtitled foreign language series and movies are aired frequently. Satellite dishes are becoming increasingly common. Most apartment buildings are festooned with devices to pick up foreign programming.

In a 1997 survey by MediaTech Ltd, it was found that over 44% of the people spent one to three hours a day watching television. Over 31% spent more than three hours a day on television. The most popular television programming format was the news (69% viewership) followed by Taiwanese dramas (56%) and Mandarin variety shows (39%).

Cable television has made significant inroads in Taiwan, especially in northern and central Taiwan. Penetration rates for cable television range from 59% of households in southern Taiwan up to 70% in the Taichung area. Sixty-two percent of the cable systems offer more than 35 channels. Prior to 1993, when Taiwan's Cable Television Law went into effect, television advertising went exclusively to the three broadcast networks. The expansion of cable television and satellite broadcasting has not only checked advertising investment in the three networks but the low cost-per-thousand viewers on cable has led many advertisers to use cable on a regular basis. About 10% of television advertising billings in 1995 for local advertising agencies was generated through cable television and satellite broadcasting.

Newspapers The most popular advertising medium in Taiwan is the island's 60 daily newspapers and the 200 weekly and monthly newspapers. Total circulation is around 6 million. Over 40% of total advertising spending is used on newspapers. Taiwan's largest newspapers are *Central Daily News, China Times* and *United Daily News*.

Newspaper readership is high in Taiwan. According to a 1997 GIO report, over 50% of the people read one newspaper each day and 12% read at least two newspapers a day. Only 21% of the population does not read newspapers.

Taiwan's major advertisers often utilise the lower-circulation newspapers in medium-sized cities to supplement their advertising in the large-circulation national dailies. When buying advertising space in the dailies, be sure their circulation claims are audited by the Audit Bureau Corporation (ABC) or other independent auditing agency. Some Taiwanese newspapers run different editions on the same day with different advertisements in each edition. This makes it a nightmare for advertisers, who do not know exactly where their advertisements run or who sees them.

The two main English language dailies, *China News* and *China Post,* reach both the expatriate community and Taiwanese professionals who read English. *Business Taiwan*, an English-language weekly, is targeted at the business community and covers domestic business and economic news.

Magazines More than 3,000 periodicals are published in Taiwan. Advertising in Taiwanese magazines is approaching 10% of all advertising expenditure in the country. The most widely circulated magazine in Taiwan is the Chinese-language edition of the *Reader's Digest*. A 1997 survey by MediaTech Ltd reported that about 30% of the population read magazines occasionally and 8% read one magazine periodically. However, almost 60% of the people claimed that they did not read magazines. Advertisers use speciality magazines to reach niche markets. For example, advertisers wishing to reach executives advertise in *Commonwealth*, a popular management magazine in Taiwan. One of the most comprehensive listing of Taiwan's many niche publications can be found on the Internet.

Radio   There are more radio stations per capita in Taiwan than in any other country in the world. As a result, Taiwan's radio market is highly segmented, with many stations specialising in news, Chinese rock, foreign rock and classical music, among others. Even with almost 180 radio stations on the island, only 8% of advertising spending is directed their way. One station in Taipei, International Community Radio (ICRT), covers interesting news features for the expatriate community and is very popular with local Chinese.

Surveys show that the Taiwanese market is split almost equally among those who listen to radio (33%), those who listen occasionally (34%) and those who do not listen to radio (32%).

Direct Mail   Direct mail advertising is becoming more common in Taiwan but is still in the developmental stage. There are projections of sizeable growth in the direct mail industry for the next few years due to increasing numbers of women entering the job market and who therefore have less time to do traditional comparison shopping for their families. Marketers who want to reach their female customers must be more aggressive in promoting awareness of their brands.

Cinema   Taiwanese audiences have long been used to commercials before movies in cinemas. While the audience waits for the movie to start, they are treated to advertising strips and stills. Cinema advertising is useful in reaching young audiences, but demographic information on viewership is sketchy. Advertising expenditure in cinemas is less than 1% of total media expenditure.

Advertising Regulations
Taiwan's advertising is regulated by GIO and broadcast advertising by all stations must be authorised by GIO. Broadcast advertisements must be examined by GIO and an application, together with the advertising film, sound tape, video tape, picture cards, slides and examining fee, should be filed with GIO by the

station or the producer of the advertisement. After GIO approval, the advertisement cannot be changed.

Packaging and Printing

As Taiwan developed its exporting prowess, it also developed its printing and packaging capabilities. It has never made sense to put a good product in a poor-quality package. The demands of the sophisticated international market required Taiwan's exporters to use quality packaging and printing to meet international standards. A modern package design and printing industry developed in Taiwan to satisfy manufacturers' needs.

Packaging services in Taiwan have become so sophisticated and comparatively inexpensive that many foreign manufacturers have their packages created in Taiwan. If you are selling to the Taiwan market, it will probably make sense to have your product package designed and packaged (or re-packaged) in Taiwan. Printers and packagers are more willing to accept small runs than is generally the case elsewhere.

Public Relations

In recent years, Taiwan has been a growing market for the public relations industry. Both domestic and international corporations have channelled some expenditure from traditional advertising into public relations, as well as into direct and promotional marketing.

Taiwan's domestic and foreign public relations firms have become sophisticated and offer services to foreign corporations that sponsor sports events, school improvement projects and other projects that help the community and, in turn, enhance the company's corporate image.

Corporations that do not heed consumer demands for corporate involvement in community projects and events can suffer a loss of support and brand loyalty. Companies that support a community's school events (both academic and sports), professional sports teams or cultural events will be appreciated by consumers. One soft drink company earned considerable goodwill in one Taiwanese city when it sponsored the refurbishment of the city's landmark opera house.

Personal Selling

Buyer and Seller Relationships
The buyer is king in Taiwan. Competition is fierce and sellers, in most sectors at least, must be more courteous and more service-oriented than their competitors. This creates a situation that many buyers take advantage of to inflict maximum humiliation on the desperate seller.

Buyers and customers, in general, expect not only excellent service but "favours" as well. Corporate buyers expect freebies such as sports event tickets, gifts for their families and other tokens of appreciation in exchange for their business. Compliments to sellers for excellent service are rare since customers consider such service as their due.

Gift-giving and excellent service are ways of creating obligations. The seller hopes the gifts he or she lavishes upon the buyer will create a feeling of indebtedness in the buyer that will influence his or her next buying decision. Indebtedness is serious business in Chinese culture. A recipient of goodwill who does not return a favour loses the respect of others.

Trade Shows
The China External Trade Development Council (CETRA) organises most of the large international trade shows and exhibitions in Taiwan. CETRA stages about 25 trade shows each year at the Taipei World Trade Centre (TWTC) Exhibition Hall. Most are annual events. The normal line-up looks like this:

- Showcase of Taiwan Products
- Taipei Aerospace Technology Exhibition

The Taipei World Trade Centre's exhibition hall puts up over 12 major industry trade shows each year.

- Taipei Computer Application Show
- Taipei International Audio/Video Electronics & Multi-Media Show
- Taipei International Auto & Motorcycle Parts & Accessories Show
- Taipei International Computer Show (Computex Taipei)
- Taipei International Construction & Building Materials Show (Taipei Build)
- Taipei International Cycle Show
- Taipei International Electronics Show
- Taipei International Flower Show
- Taipei International Food Industry Show
- Taipei International Furniture Show
- Taipei International Gift and Stationery Autumn Show
- Taipei International Gift & Stationery Spring Show (GIFTIONERY)

- Taipei International Jewellery & Timepiece Show
- Taipei International Leather Goods Show
- Taipei International Machine Tool Show (TIMTOS)
- Taipei International Plastic & Rubber Show (TAIPEI PLAS)
- Taipei International Toy Show

Using Translators and Interpreters

For a marketing campaign in Taiwan, Pepsi used a translated version of the slogan, "Come alive with the Pepsi Generation" that appeared in Chinese as "Pepsi will bring your ancestors back from the dead". In a similar mishap, a Kentucky Fried Chicken translation of "Finger-lickin' good" came out as "Eat your fingers off"!

Foreign executives who visit a Taiwanese company will find that there will likely be an interpreter present in the meeting. This is true even if the heads of the company speak English. The interpreter is usually an in-house staff interpreter, but occasionally, an outside interpreter from an agency is hired. Even so, the foreign executive should bring his or her own interpreter to the meeting as a matter of courtesy and as a wise business practice.

Do not bring along an unqualified interpreter. Your interpreter's ability can make or break some deals or relationships. However, determining the quality of interpreters is not easy if you do not speak Chinese. The best way to screen potential interpreters is to get recommendations from others more familiar with Taiwan. Ask expatriate business people who have been in Taiwan for some time for their recommendations. Local Chinese business people, not connected with your potential business partner, can also offer referrals.

To ensure that you obtain the services of a qualified interpreter, interview and engage him or her as far in advance as possible. The best ones are in demand and not easy to book—especially if they are specialists in technical, industry-specific jargon. This will also allow time for you to get your company information and the topic of discussion to the interpreter in advance. Giving your interpreter a chance to prepare will enhance your chances of a smooth and effective meeting.

The standard charge for interpretation is from NT$3,000–NT$10,000 (US$88–US$294) per day, depending on the skill and experience of the interpreter. Most interpreters and agencies charge by the day or half-day since the interpreter cannot easily commit to two clients on the same day. Thus, even if the actual meeting is only 2 or 3 hours long, expect to pay for at least half a day.

Translators, on the other hand, usually charge on a per-page basis. As with interpreters, the fee rate varies with the skill of (and demand for) the translator. A normal one-page business letter will cost about NT$500 to translate from English to Chinese. For highly sensitive documents or publications, it is advisable to have a second translator check the accuracy of the first translator's work. By getting a second opinion, one foreign chamber of commerce avoided having their organisation described as the Ministry of Economic Affairs throughout their Chinese-language brochure.

Try to find a translator who does not translate word-by-word. Translations should first be localised into the target language. Some US translators, for example, do this by recreating the document inspired by the original. Because of the drastic grammar differences between English and Chinese, each sentence and paragraph is rewritten to match the intended meaning of the original. The recreated document should then be reviewed by a bilingual editor for accuracy and then checked by a proofreader to ensure seamless flow and agreement with the meaning of the original.

Using Local Representatives

While only the largest companies can contemplate a permanent presence in the Taiwanese market, having local representation is a critical factor for success in Taiwan. The Taiwanese do not like to do business with strangers. It is not common for Taiwanese companies to buy anything from someone they do not know.

What to Look For in a Taiwanese Agent/Distributor

- A good reputation with suppliers, banks and customers
- Chinese and English language ability
- Experience with the Taiwanese market
- An established sales organisation and trained staff
- Experience with relevant product lines
- Adequate financial strength
- Reasonable representative's fees
- After-sales service capabilities
- A good reputation with other clients

The choice of local representation is also critical. Spend the necessary time and money to identify and engage your representation in Taiwan because in the long run, it is your representative that will either make you or break you in the market.

The quality of a representative's contacts will often be a more important selling point than the intrinsic marketability of your product. Introductions are vital: "cold calling" is not the way to start a business relationship in Taiwan.

The "Classmate Network"
The "classmate network" is an invisible yet crucial part of business in Taiwan. School ties are very important and long lasting for the Taiwanese. Whether it is a senior government official, an executive of a major corporation or an academic, the contacts developed at school or university carry over into later careers in a way not found in the West. A representative who graduated from a prestigious university or military school will have a ready-made network to tap into on your behalf.

Finding a Qualified Agent or Distributor
Too many foreign manufacturers and exporters have made the mistake of not checking up on foreign agents or distributors before

signing a contract for representation. One US medical equipment manufacturer signed an exclusive distribution agreement for the "Asia-Pacific region" with a Taipei-based medical equipment distributor that did not have a network developed outside of Taipei, much less the Asia-Pacific region. The US firm had received an inquiry from the Taipei distributor and had signed an agreement without even checking their claims or visiting Taiwan. The US company eventually had to buy off the Taipei distributor to get out of the contract.

Outright misrepresentation of abilities is not uncommon among those claiming to be agents or distributors. Do take a look for yourself. Otherwise, you are simply asking for trouble.

Spend Time with Your Representative
Having a representative is very much like being married. If you do not put time and effort into it, you drift apart, sometimes amicably, but more often than not, in acrimony. Taiwan is a geographically small place and everyone eventually hears about caustic separations.

Beware of the Gracious Host
In his talks to Australian business people, Peter Osborne, executive director of the Australian Business Centre in Taiwan, tells them to be wary of prospective representatives and companies that want to dominate their time. "Particularly the ones that pick you up from the airport, wine and dine you for three days and put you on the plane back home", says Osborne. "That way, you think you've had a wonderful time but you haven't had a chance to meet anyone else or get any other views on the market, your product or your business strategy."

Importing Into Taiwan

The Import Licensing System

There are two types of importable goods in Taiwan: controlled and permissible items. Taiwan used to be rife with import bans and restrictions, but it has moved to liberalise its trading system in its campaign to be admitted to the WTO. More and more goods are finding their way off the banned or restricted lists onto the permissible items list.

There are 9,053 items on the tariff rate system, of which only 242 are controlled. However, 35% of the importable items require a permit prior to importation. About 699 items require prior

---

Tariff Rates

As a rule of thumb, the basic tariff rate for most items is as follows:

• Raw materials	0–2.5%
• Semi-processed goods	0–10%
• Finished goods	5–15%

For a few selected items, the tariff rates average as follows:

• Mineral products	0–20%
• Chemical products	0.1–10%
• Raw leather	0–10%
• Synthetic rubber material	0–10%
• Wood and wood products	0–20%
• Concrete	0–30%
• Glass	0–30%
• Precious metals	0–20%
• Machinery	0–30%
• Airplanes	0–50%
• Autos	30–40%

---

approval from BOFT and another 2,194 items require permits from banks and other BOFT-licensed organisations.

Import Duties

Taiwan's tariff rate system is based on the Harmonised Commodity Description and Coding System (HS) used by most countries. The HS code for your product must be used in the import documentation. The tariff rate system and the applied duties are overseen by MOF's Department of Customs Administration.

The ROC government has fallen behind on its targets for its tariff-cutting programme but has made significant reductions in the rates for industrial products. The nominal rates in this category were a little over 6% in 1997.

Taiwan's tariff rates are generally ad valorem and based on the CIF (Cost, Insurance, Freight) value. For goods that are imported at very low prices, the local market value can be used as the basis for determining the duty payable.

No duty is charged on incoming parcels containing gifts or personal items valued under NT$6,000 or advertising materials or samples valued under NT$12,000.

In general, duties on imported essential machinery is either much reduced or 0%. If machinery and equipment qualify as essential for certain high-tech industries covered by the Statute for Industrial Upgrading, no duties will be levied on their importation. Industries that qualify include those in electrical engineering, electronics, machinery manufacturing, shipbuilding, chemicals, steel, aluminium, copper, textile dyeing and mining.

In Taiwan, you can phone the Duty Information Centre with any duty-related question. Other information on duty rates can be obtained from the Ministry of Finance's Directorate General of Customs. English language copies of Taiwan's Customs Import Tariff and Classification Schedule can be obtained from CETRA.

Prohibited Items
Items that cannot be imported into Taiwan include:

- Obscene books, videos, magazines, etc.
- Counterfeit money or bank and security notes
- Foreign lottery tickets or gambling tools
- Pro-communist literature
- Firearms or ammunition
- Illegal drugs such as marijuana, opium, cocaine, etc.
- Toy guns and gun-shaped items
- Articles infringing the rights of trademarks, copyrights and patents
- Endangered wildlife species and/or their products
- Animals, soil or plants from areas affected by injurious pests and diseases

Duty-related Fees

A commodity tax ranging from 2% to 60% ad valorem is charged if an imported item falls into certain commodity categories.

Taiwan charges a harbour construction fee—0.5% of declared value—on all goods arriving by sea.

Import Financing

If you are importing high-tech equipment into Taiwan, your Taiwanese customer may be eligible for import financing from the Export-Import Bank of the ROC. The Export-Import Bank provides loans of up to 85% of the total contract value for equipment that will improve the efficiency and technology base of Taiwanese companies or for equipment used in the manufacture of goods for export. Loans are also available for importers of raw materials, spare parts or natural resources.

Where to Find Help

Industry Trade Associations

Every industry in Taiwan has its own trade association. Everyone, from the glove manufacturers to the plastic Christmas tree manufacturers, has their association. While most of these organisations are export-oriented, they do provide varying degrees of assistance to foreign business people. If you are searching for sources of components these companies specialise in, you can contact them. If you want your product assembled in Taiwan, you can start your search for a business partner from the list of members in the relevant association.

A list of many of these trade associations is included in appendix B of this book. For a more comprehensive list, you can contact CETRA.

The China External Trade Development Council (CETRA)

As outlined in chapter 3, CETRA is a semi-governmental organisation supported by business associations and exporters— much like the Korea Trade Association (KOTRA) or Singapore's Trade Development Board (TDB). Listed below are some of the services provided by CETRA:

- Sponsoring trade shows in Taiwan and organising overseas exhibitions and missions
- Publishing the latest information on foreign buyers, Taiwanese importers, exporters and suppliers, as well as trade statistics and customs information
- Publishing trade journals featuring Taiwan's products and market conditions
- Providing trade development assistance through CETRA's many overseas representative offices

CETRA can be contacted through its overseas offices or at its headquarters.

The Taipei World Trade Centre (TWTC):

TWTC is a sister organisation of CETRA. Founded in 1980, TWTC is a member of the New York-based World Trade Centres Association. Its exhibition hall has been managed by CETRA since its completion in 1986. A total of 163,000 sq. m of exhibition space is available on seven levels of its facility. The 26,886-sq.-m ground floor alone provides enough space for 1,313 temporary trade show booths.

On the second through sixth floors of the exhibition hall, TWTC maintains a permanent export mart consisting of 898 showrooms, each of them 40 sq. m in area. The export mart is divided on the basis of 14 product categories, such as electronics and jewellery, and all showrooms are staffed by sales people from the exhibiting firms. There is also an export product display centre on the second floor, with more than 1,500 unmanned exhibits of various sizes.

The Taipei World Trade Centre complex also includes a 34-storey International Trade Building (ITB). The building's 34 stories and three basement levels are home to many international organisations. The top two levels of the ITB are devoted to the TWTC Club, part of the World Trade Centre Association's international club network.

China Economic News Service (CENS)

CENS publishes a wide range of publications about Taiwan's industries and market conditions. CENS was founded in 1974 as an affiliate of the United Daily News Group, Taiwan's largest newspaper conglomerate. Besides publishing trade journals, CENS also engages in a variety of trade-related services. CENS acts as the sales agent in Taiwan for many international trade fairs and trade magazines. On behalf of CETRA, CENS publishes a directory of all CETRA-organised international trade fairs in Taiwan. Among the trade journals published by CENS are:

- Taiwan Machinery
- Taiwan Lighting
- Taiwan Hardware
- Taiwan Furniture
- Taiwan Transportation Equipment Guide (TTG)
- Mercancia de Taiwan
- Taiwan Export Express
- Taiwan Electronics
- Taiwan Computer Guide
- Taiwan Industrial Suppliers (TIS)
- Directory of Taiwan's Leading Manufacturers & Exporters (TAIMEX)
- Directory of ISO Certified Companies in Taiwan

CENS also organises groups of Taiwanese manufacturers to attend foreign exhibitions. CENS maintains a home page as well as a free searchable directory of Taiwanese corporations on the Internet.

Potential Markets in Taiwan

When determining the prospects for your product in the Taiwanese market (or any other market for that matter), it is wise to first look at the total market size for the product category as well as the market's total imports in that category. By so doing, you will be able to surmise, among other things, if the local industry is protected from foreign competition or if the market is open to imports of a certain product category. The table below gives an idea of the potential of several product categories in Taiwan:

The opportunities in Taiwan vary according to product category, and this is more so within product categories. What follows is a brief synopsis of the characteristics of several promising market categories in Taiwan.

Market Size and Import Totals for Selected Product Categories (1997)*

Product Category	Total Market Size (local consumption)	Total Imports
Electronic components	29,058	17,151
Computers/Accessories	3,909	2,576
Household consumer goods	3,795	1,192
Scientific instruments	2,581	2,505
Industrial process controls	2,284	2,178
Telecommunications equipment	1,790	1,185
Pumps, valves and compressors	1,294	1,013
Cosmetics/Toiletries	677	448
Pollution control equipment	629	824
Medical equipment	529	385

* All figures in US$ billion.

Source: Board of Foreign Trade

Computers and Accessories

The market for computers and accessories is booming. Despite intense competition from Taiwan's own computer manufacturers, there are opportunities for foreign companies who are strong in the market niche. The rapid growth of Internet usage and the education system's extensive training programmes are creating rapid growth in computer sales and services. Corporations, schools and research institutes are rapidly expanding their investments in computerisation and networking systems.

In 1997, Taiwan imported US$2.57 billion worth of computer equipment and exported US$17.7 billion.

Electronic Components

Taiwan's electronic manufacturers import significant amounts of components, such as integrated circuits (IC), for assembly into their equipment. The more electronic equipment Taiwan produces, the more leading-edge components it imports. In 1997, Taiwan imported US$17.15 billion worth of electronic components.

Telecommunications Equipment and Services

During the 1990s, Taiwan upgraded its telecommunications infrastructure, creating new opportunities for foreign manufacturers and service providers. Liberalisation of the Taiwanese market is expected to provide sales opportunities in the mobile phone, satellite network services, as well as domestic and international phone service areas in the coming years.

Industrial Process Controls

Taiwan's labour shortage and drive to modernise its production efficiency make the importation of leading-edge industrial process controls a necessity. The authorities have enacted various tax incentives to encourage its manufacturers to purchase modern production equipment and therefore upgrade their production ability. Taiwan imports almost all of the industrial process controls it uses.

Travel and Tourism Services

Taiwanese travel abroad is booming. In 1997, the total number of trips abroad by ROC citizens was more than 25% of the island's population. Most Taiwanese travel to Asian destinations, such as mainland China, the Philippines and Singapore. Outside of Asia, the United States is the most popular tourist destination. Taiwan's travel agents are scrambling to offer more attractive tour packages in the increasingly competitive Taiwanese market.

Pollution Control Equipment

While implementation of Taiwan's increasingly stringent environmental laws were relaxed in 1997 due to the Asian financial crisis (and the subsequent economic strains), many observers expect sales of pollution control equipment (PCE) to continue to grow at a rate of about 5% per year. Taiwan suffered the negative consequences of uncontrolled industrial growth and lax pollution control during the 1970s and 1980s. By the early 1990s, however, the authorities had enacted tough environmental laws to clean up the mess. Taiwan became a great market for producers of pollution control equipment. Some of the imported equipment are used as components in manufactured goods exported by the country.

Education and Training

Foreign universities and schools can attract Taiwanese students and corporate staff for higher training. Since Taiwan relaxed its rules governing studying abroad in 1989, growing numbers of Taiwan's affluent families have sent their children abroad for university education. Short-term language study is in high demand. In 1997, the Taiwanese spent US$1.2 billion educating their children abroad, mostly in the United States (45%).

Cosmetics and Toiletries

Taiwan's increasing affluence and rising living standards have given rise to a growing consumer market for cosmetics and toiletries. Taiwanese consumers prize foreign brands and imports of such products have been averaging close to 10% annually since 1995. Imported cosmetics and toiletries made up 66% of the total Taiwanese market in this product category in 1997.

Selling Food Products to Taiwan

Historically, Taiwan has been very protective of its domestic food industry. Farmers and food processors have benefited from a wide range of protective measures, including outright bans on the importation of competing products and high tariffs for processed foods. Taiwan's peanut growers, for example, are protected by a ban on foreign peanut imports. Although all other types of nuts (pistachios, cashews, etc.) are imported because they cannot be grown in Taiwan, the local food processors are protected by high tariffs on imported processed foods. Therefore, most nuts are imported in a raw state and de-shelled, roasted, flavoured and packaged in Taiwan to take advantage of the significantly lower tariff on unprocessed nuts. As a result, at the retail level, foreign brands of nuts, such as Planters, are priced much higher than locally processed nuts.

Distribution Sub-markets

There are basically three distribution sub-markets for processed foods in Taiwan. These include:

- Retail Outlets
- Restaurants
- Food Manufacturers

For snack foods, very popular among the Chinese, the karaoke night clubs (KTV) are an important fourth sub-market.

Retail outlets account for the largest percentage of sales for most imported processed foods. The retail outlet sub-market consists of six types of outlets. They are:

- Hypermarkets
- Supermarkets
- Convenience Stores (CVS)
- Government Discount Stores
- Specialty Food Stores
- Street markets

The hypermarket channel of distribution opened up in Taiwan in the late 1980s with the introduction of several hypermarket retail outlet stores. This type of high-volume discounted price outlet is a growing concept in Taiwan. The Carrefour and Makro hypermarket chains, in particular, offer consumers the opportunity to purchase most varieties of imported and domestic foods.

While hypermarkets island-wide currently represent a small percentage of the total food market, they are expected to continue to expand throughout the island, offering Taiwanese consumers an additional source for buying food items.

There are approximately five major supermarket chains with an estimated 400–500 locations island-wide. They consist of the following companies:

- Wellcome
- Matsusei
- Kasumi
- Park N Shop
- Hypermart

Convenience stores are a major outlet for many processed food items and are highly prevalent in Taipei and northern Taiwan but less so in southern Taiwan. The following convenience store chains are currently operating in Taiwan:

- 7-11
- O.K.
- Family Mart
- AM PM
- Nikomart
- Hi-Life

The central government operates over 500 discount stores for the exclusive use of military personnel, civil servants and teachers. These outlets provide the same services as hypermarkets, but the prices average 25% less than supermarket prices.

Specialty food stores are catching on in Taiwan. These are outlets that specialise in a niche food market—usually a high value-

Foreign business people can learn about Taiwanese buying habits and sales techniques at Taiwan's many street markets.

added line of related items. Nu-Sun, or "Hsin Tung Yang", for example, specialises in expensive snack foods (nuts, meat jerkies, dried fish, shrimp crackers, etc.) Taiwanese love to eat while drinking alcohol.

Street markets are found in most Taiwanese neighbourhoods, even affluent neighbourhoods. These predecessors of the modern grocery supermarkets still offer a wide variety of fresh vegetables, fruit, meats and other sundries. Foods sold at the street market are sold in bulk by the kilogram. Housewives or domestic help can buy anything from a head of *bokchoy* lettuce to many kilograms of fresh fish at these lively markets.

Food Distribution Channels

Many Taiwanese food importers employ duel channels of distribution. Since the tariff rates on imported processed foods are still much higher than the tariff on unprocessed food imports,

·

many importers opt to process foods after importing them to Taiwan. The importer then sells directly to the larger retail outlets and food manufacturers. The other popular channel importers follow is to sell directly to a distributor who, in turn, sells directly to the more remote retail outlets and food manufacturers.

Profit Margins
Profit margins in the processed foods industries vary widely, but average profit margins for most importers and retailers are around 20%. When distributors are used, importer profit margins are generally split with the distributor for equal 10% mark-ups.

Packaging Requirements
Exporters of processed food products to Taiwan must adhere to the following labelling requirements:

In addition to the manufacturer's original foreign language label, each product must also have a clearly legible label in Chinese containing the following information:

- Ingredients
- Weight
- Manufacturer's and importer's full company name
- Expiration date
- Shelf life/best before date

Miscellaneous Fees
In addition to tariffs, there are several miscellaneous fees food importers and exporters should take note of:

- Harbour construction fee: 0.5 % of CIF price
- Trade promotion fee: 0.05 % of CIF price
- Customs clearance fee per shipment: NT$500
- Disease inspection fee: varies as a percentage of CIF price

The ROC Department of Health tests the first shipment of a new food product that arrives in Taiwan. After the initial test, shipments will be tested randomly.

Chapter 7

Protocol for Correspondence and Meetings

Business Correspondence

It is easy to reach anyone anywhere in Taiwan by phone, but there is still good reason to use the written word in business communications. The advantage of postal mail, fax or e-mail is that it creates a record and conveys information. Information frozen on the page can be readily analysed and reviewed by the recipient—a benefit to those who must operate in a language other than their own. Taiwanese business people usually communicate with foreigners in English, but they are more comfortable with reading English than speaking it.

It is also considered proper to request a meeting with a stranger in written form before calling him or her by telephone or dropping by personally. A well thought-out formal letter requesting a meeting and stating your reason for wanting to meet will get the recipient's consideration and has a better chance of getting you in the door. If you follow up with a telephone call, your Taiwanese counterpart will at least have had a chance to read your proposal and be better prepared to respond.

Titles and proper use of names are very important to the Taiwanese. When addressing high ranking executives or government officials, it is appropriate to address them using their title and family name. For example, if you are writing to a company

---

Communication Tip

Do not use red ink to write notes or letters in Taiwan. Red ink conveys an unfriendly meaning.

chairman called Sun Wei-chen, you should address him as "Chairman Sun".

The following points will help you format your formal correspondence appropriately:

- Use a company letterhead to establish authority.
- The address should be accompanied by the recipient's full name and title.
- Use the recipient's title and family name in the salutation. If you do not know the person's name, use "Dear Sir or Madam".

To create a good impression and to communicate your ideas in a clear and concise manner, you should:

- Start your letter or fax with a courteous greeting and end with a friendly closing. Do not be abrupt. Request assistance graciously and do not assume that it will be forthcoming.
- Close your letter or fax with a friendly statement such as "Looking forward to seeing you soon".
- Avoid using idioms or slang. Do not use big words if a simple word can be used. Even if the recipient speaks English well, you can reduce the chance of misunderstandings by using simple, straightforward language.
- Reread your completed letter from the point of view of the intended recipient with a not too perfect command of English. Have a co-worker read your letter to see if you are conveying your intentions clearly.
- If you are still not getting an answer to your letters or faxes after sending it a few times, try re-addressing it to someone else in his/her company or resend the letter and "cc" it to the recipient's boss. If the recipient sees that you have sent it to his/her boss, he/she will be more likely to reply.

The following page shows a sample fax:

Greyman Enterprises, Inc.

January 22, 1998

To: Mr Harvey Chang
            Chairman
            Radiant Technology Research Co.

From: Mr Greg Silva
            Director
            Greyman Enterprises, Inc.

Dear Chairman Chang,

I am very pleased to receive your fax of January 20, and to learn of your upcoming visit to Oklahoma City. Please accept my warmest welcome.

I have taken the liberty to reserve 2.00–3.00 p.m. on February 2 (Thursday) for you and Mr Sun to meet in my office at this address: 7th floor, 900 N. Stiles Street, Oklahoma City. I know your schedule is tight and so hope the scheduled meeting is alright with you. Please inform me of your flight arrival details so we can meet you at Will Rogers Airport.

Looking forward to seeing you soon.

Sincerely,

Greg Silva

700 N. Greenwood, Tulsa, Oklahoma 74102 USA

Responding to Communications

Answer inquiries, proposals, correspondence and invitations as soon as possible. At the very least, send an acknowledgement stating that an answer will follow shortly. The pace of business in Taiwan demands speedy action. Prompt responses in communicating with business associates in Taiwan indicates professionalism, commitment and an interest in the market.

Addresses and Titles

Use titles both in written and spoken communications. Letters should be addressed using titles and honorifics, as in:

> Mr. Harvey Chang
> Chairman
> Radiant Technology Research Inc.
> 333 Keelung St.
> Taipei, Taiwan

If you are sending correspondence to an agency of the ROC national government, use "Taiwan, ROC" in the address.

While formality is the rule in written communications, in person or on the phone, most Taiwanese are straightforward and are sometimes even blunt. It is easy to misinterpret meanings and moods when talking over the phone. Keep in mind that your Taiwanese counterpart is not operating in his or her native language (unless you are using Taiwanese) and allow plenty of room for miscommunication. Speak simply and directly, and avoid colloquialisms.

In Person

Introductions

People should be introduced in order of rank, beginning with those with the highest rank and proceeding to the lowest. Do not introduce people using only their given names because this is considered too informal. "May I introduce Mr Wei-Jing Bai?" is correct. "May I introduce Wei-Jing" is not. The Taiwanese only use given names among close friends and relatives. Even among Taiwanese who have lived in the United States for years, the use of given names is reserved for friends and family.

The Business Card

Taiwanese business people always exchange name cards, or *mingpian*, when they meet for the first time. The mingpian is an important means of identification. Business people keep card files of mingpian for reference and as an address book of sorts. After a meeting (not during), many Taiwanese business people note relevant information about people they have met on the back of each card received. If you know that you will be seeing the person again at an upcoming event or meeting, it will be helpful to review the person's card and any notes on it prior to seeing them. When you see them again, mention that you remember meeting them and include a titbit of information that will impress upon them that you do indeed recall meeting them. If your notes include a mention that the other person's child had attended the same university as your child, then mentioning that fact again will give your Taiwanese counterpart the feeling that he/she had enough of an impact on you to cause you to remember him/her and that which is important to him/her. The more you review your card collection, the more you will remember about your contacts.

Most Taiwan business people you meet will be able to speak or read English fairly well. However, it is polite to have bilingual business cards prepared (Chinese on one side and English on the other) for use in Taiwan or when meeting business people from Taiwan. Either have these bilingual cards printed locally before you travel to Taiwan or have them done immediately upon arrival in Taiwan. The advantage to having it done upon arrival in Taiwan by an experienced translation and printing firm is the higher likelihood that the translation and printing will be done according to Taiwanese standards and language usage.

Some print shops in the larger cities can translate and print bilingual mingpian in a matter of hours. The business centres in the finer hotels can handle this for you. To speed up the process, fax an enlarged copy of your business card to the hotel before your arrival and ask them to have their business centre arrange it to be translated by professionals before your arrival. It is usually possible to have the Taiwanese translation printed on the blank side of your existing cards. Bring enough cards with you for this purpose. If you prefer to have the entire card printed in Taiwan, be sure to bring "camera-ready" company logo art with you.

Do not skimp on paper and printing quality. A poor quality card will send the wrong impression. Use fine quality paper, preferably a heavy white stock, with black letters/characters. Engraved printing, embossing and gold logos or edging are quality touches that will lend elegance and sophistication. Most business cards in Taiwan include the organisation's logo on the card.

In Taiwan, it is also customary to include all your titles in one card. If, for example, Dr Chien Liu is the president of his own computer company as well as the chairman of the Taipei Computer Association, he will include his association title on his company business card. If your academic degree is relevant to your business, include it on your card as well. If you hold a doctorate, add "PhD." on your card so others will know the proper honorific.

Keep your business cards in special card cases in your jacket pocket or purse for easy handling. It is poor form to fish for your card in pants pockets or in a wallet mixed with credit cards, etc.

In addition to your name, business cards should include your position, company name, logo, address, telephone number, fax number and e-mail address. Take twice as many cards with you to Taiwan as you think you would use, for almost every business contact involves the exchange of mingpian. Cards are also often enclosed with correspondence.

Mingpian Etiquette

When meeting someone, offer them your business card with both hands and bow or dip your head forward to show respect. If you are introduced in Chinese, present your card Chinese-side up so that it is easily readable to the person receiving it. If you are introduced in English—presumably because the Taiwanese person understands English—present your card with the English side up. This will acknowledge the recipient's English language ability. The host should offer his card first.

Shaking hands is not a Taiwanese custom, but some Taiwanese business people will willingly attempt it. If they do not offer their hand, simply bow slightly. If you are uncertain whether to bow or shake hands, bow first and then offer to shake hands. Many Taiwanese have perfected a handshake-and-bow combo when greeting Westerners.

The Taiwanese do not like a firm handshake. While this is good form in some cultures, the Taiwanese consider it aggressive. Keep the grip relaxed and do not pump the other person's arm up and down. Do not try to grab an arm or elbow in an effort to be friendly as this is just too much touching for the Taiwanese—especially among the older, more conservative Taiwanese.

In group situations that include Westerners, the accommodating Taiwanese will usually shake hands all around and then present business cards. The typical Taiwanese procedure, however, would be to bow first and then exchange cards. The presentation of cards is the formal act of greeting.

Foreigners not used to bowing can meet the Taiwanese halfway by giving this form of respect a try. For the novice, a short bow is adequate. As you become more comfortable with it, a bow with the body bent at about 15 degrees and held for about two seconds is appropriate. Taiwanese men bow with their hands at their sides and fingers resting on the seams of their trousers. Women place their hands on the front of their thighs and bow. At departure, the Taiwanese will give several brief bows.

While extended eye contact is considered a sign of trust and openness in the West, the Taiwanese consider it rude and threatening. For Westerners used to staring into their counterparts' eyes during a prolonged discussion, you could make it easier for yourself by periodically looking over your Taiwanese counterparts' shoulders or at their throats for short intervals.

Do not take someone's card and casually put it aside. Remember that to the Taiwanese, the card is a representation of its owner. To treat the card with disrespect is to treat its owner with disrespect. It is an insult to take someone's card and casually place it in a pocket as if the card and the person it represents are not important. Accept the card with both hands and a slight bow, read the card and offer some social pleasantry, addressing the person by title and name. Show, with an expression of interest, that you are impressed with the title and organisation of the person you are meeting.

The business card provides clues about a person you are meeting for the first time and the Taiwanese are adept at understanding them. They read business cards very carefully for indications of rank. The Taiwanese culture is a hierarchical one and Taiwanese place great importance on relative ranks within organisations. The information on a card can also provide a starting point for conversations. A card might show, for example, that the person's office is located in a prestigious section of Taipei and this fact can be mentioned during the conversation.

During the greeting and card exchange process, do not try to engage in a lot of verbal patter. Give the other party the chance to absorb the information on the business cards. Trying to lighten the situation with superfluous pleasantries about the weather, current events or traffic will distract from the job at hand—sizing up one another. The Taiwanese are not nearly as uncomfortable as Westerners are with periods of silence. After the cards and greetings have been exchanged, light social conversation can lead into the business discussion.

The Taiwanese have a most useful habit of placing the business cards of those they have just met on the table in front of them so they can refer to them during the conversation. They usually arrange the cards in the order the people are seated so they can connect the names with the owners. Since foreign names may be hard to pronounce, this custom can be helpful in recalling names. I have adopted this custom for meetings throughout the world.

Do not scribble notes on someone's business card in their presence. If you place them on the table during a meeting, do not shuffle them about, set tea cups on top of them or leave them behind when you depart.

If a special title, such as doctor or minister, is used on a card, you should use this title to address the person. If it is included on the card, it must be important to the holder.

Business cards can sometimes be used as proxy in introductions. References are very important in Taiwanese society because the person who acts as the introducer accepts responsibility for the actions of those he introduces. A Taiwanese may serve as your character reference or introducer by writing a note on the back of their business card to identify you as a friend. Such a reference card can be included in correspondence or attached to the curriculum vitae when applying for a job. It is quite improper to use someone's business card in this manner without his or her permission. If you are the beneficiary of this type of business card guarantee, you should later send a note to the card owner to thank him. It would be appropriate to show appreciation with a gift.

Within the context of Taiwanese society, the person who holds another person's business card has some claim on him or her. It is wise to hand out your name cards only to those with whom you wish to have a relationship. It is not wise to stick your card onto every piece of company literature sent out.

Business over Lunch?

The Taiwanese are not given to long, chatty lunches—or even business lunches. The rank and file gobble noodles and return to work. Clerks tend to eat at their desks and continue working, seemingly chained to their desks. Executives also tend to eat simple, noodle or rice dishes and head right back to the job. There are some who still partake in that wonderful habit of bygone Taiwan—the two-hour lunch and nap.

The long business lunch where co-workers socialise at leisure or business people meet with customers is not common in Taiwan. The evening dinner and after-dinner drinks is where Taiwanese business people socialise. The weekday evening socialising with co-workers or business prospects keeps most business people out late on weekdays and away from their families.

How to Be a Good Guest

Taiwanese hosts like to take their guests to dinner. Dining out is the Taiwanese person's favourite pastime and is *de rigueur* for entertainment. Prepare for it. If you are not familiar with Taiwanese food, try it before you set foot in Taiwan. Visit local restaurants representing the many different regional cuisine of China. The Taiwanese cuisine is only one of dozens of Chinese regional cuisine. Mainlanders from all over China have settled in Taiwan and brought their restaurants with them. Taiwan is a kind of Disneyland of Chinese cuisine. Instead of "Tomorrowland" and "Frontierland", this culinary "Disneyland" offers "Hunanland" and "Sichuanland". Your host may take you to a Cantonese seafood restaurant, a Mongolian hotpot restaurant or a Beijing-style noodle restaurant. They can be as different as an Italian *trattoria* and an English pub.

The adventure of trying new foods is best approached with enthusiasm—feigned if necessary. The Taiwanese will be pleased if you show a fondness for their food. Impress them with your appreciation and knowledge of their foods and dining customs. The Taiwanese will pay attention to how a foreign guest handles

> **Eating Taiwanese-style**
> Taiwanese cuisine is similar to other eastern Chinese cooking. It has Japanese elements in it, is simple and light, and ginger is used liberally. Pork fat is often used for frying. There is an abundance of seafood. Taiwanese favourites include clams, grilled eel, turtle soup, poached shrimp and fried shrimp rolls.

his or her chopsticks. Learn to use them before you arrive in the country. Buy a pair of chopsticks and try them at home.

In many cases, your Taiwanese host will want to show you around Taiwan. You can make it easy for your host by indicating your interest in specific areas of Taiwanese culture, such as calligraphy, bronzes, tea or Taiwanese opera. Your host will likely take you to exhibitions or places related to your interests. Taiwanese hosts like to plan a full itinerary for their guests so if you do not give hints of your interests, expect to be occupied full-time doing things you may not like to do.

The National Palace Museum near Taipei is a standard stop for most Taipei-bound visitors. This is the best museum of Taiwanese art in the world and the locals are justifiably proud of it. For visitors with time for a short trip out of Taipei, Toroko Gorge and Sun Moon Lake in central Taiwan make for good visits. In southern Taiwan, the historic city of Tainan or Kenting National Park are interesting places to visit.

Seating Protocol
Anyone who has ever brought along an extra colleague to a Taiwanese-hosted banquet and witnessed the poor aides quietly scurrying around trying to adjust name cards and seating charts while the host provides conversational cover, knows how important seating is to the Taiwanese. Seating arrangements are not random.

Proper protocol requires that everyone be seated according to rank and that the host or his/her proxies direct the guests to their seats. Do not sit until invited to do so by your hosts. It is essential that the guest of honour waits to be offered the seat of honour facing the room entrance.

It is common practice in Taiwan for arriving business guests to be escorted to a "greeting" or conference room by a receptionist or junior executive. Taiwanese hosts will enter the room soon in descending order of rank. An interpreter will often assist in making the introductions. Stand as your hosts enter the room.

Seating in most greeting rooms is arranged either in a U-shape along three walls or at a conference table. At a long table, the seat of honour is the chair at the center of the table, facing the entrance. In general, the seat of honour is as far away from the room entrance as possible and faces that entrance. This custom developed from the belief that a visitor could defend himself better if he faced the entrance and could see any approaching danger. This advantageous seating arrangement came to be an indication of rank even when visitors no longer had to worry about murderous enemies lurking outside the doorway.

Exchanging Gifts

Taiwanese show respect by exchanging gifts, a practice whereby a person can unabashedly enhance his or her image. Words cannot always be taken at face value in Taiwan, but gift-giving offers a concrete way to demonstrate one's feelings of respect.

In addition to showing respect, gift-giving is also one of the best ways of entangling one another in webs of mutual indebtedness. The Taiwanese have developed this to a fine art.

Take, for example, the Taiwanese custom of giving departing friends and relatives a small gift of money for use in their travels. The travelling recipients feel such a sense of debt that they are obligated to buy souvenirs for the givers they leave behind. Thus, the vacationing Taiwanese must spend their precious holiday time searching for the perfect souvenirs for their friends and lug them back to Taiwan. If your Taiwanese friends give you departure money, do not forget to bring something back for them.

It is important to remember that if gifts are received, the goodwill must be returned in some way. Foreign business people desiring to establish business relationships with Taiwanese should be prepared to exchange many gifts. There are many rules of protocol associated with gift exchanges within Taiwanese business circles and experts and would-be experts are available to offer advice. A savvy Taiwanese secretary is the best person to give advice. Many hotel business centres can also help in this regard.

As a tradition, the host will usually thank you for your generosity but refuse to accept the gift for fear of being considered greedy if he/she takes it easily. On the other hand, the guest is supposed to insist that the host accept the gift or he/she will be considered not sincere enough. Such an "argument" might last for several rounds before the host eventually accepts the gift happily.

The host is not supposed to unwrap the gift in front of the guest. This is viewed as greedy behaviour in Taiwan.

There is a hierarchy of gift exchange. The highest ranking person should receive the best and most expensive gift. Everyone present should receive something, even if it is only a lapel pin. If you do not have enough for everyone, remember that it is better to give one significant gift to the leader of the counterpart group than to give nothing at all. This one gift is considered a symbolic gift to the entire delegation. In such a case, it is acceptable that the rest of the delegation not receive anything. It is certainly more acceptable than giving several members of the delegation a gift while leaving out a few. The best situation is, however, to have something for everyone.

As a rule of thumb, the lowest ranking member of the Taiwan team should receive a gift that is roughly half the cost of the one

Gifts for All!
I always travel with a small briefcase full of assorted gifts that I can pull out and distribute at the appropriate moment. An assortment of gifts of varying value are wrapped in easily-recognisable boxes—the contents of which I am familiar. I can easily whip out a golf putter for the president, a writing pen for the department manager and a lapel pin for the note-taker. Always bring more than you think you would possibly need. Nothing is more embarrassing than having unexpected members of the other side walk in to a meeting and you have seven gifts for eight people.

given to the leader. Your interpreter should be able to advise you on an appropriate distribution of gifts.

Do not give gifts that are too expensive. The Taiwanese will feel a need to out-spend you the next time and this could lead to a devastating escalation of gift exchanges. Gift exchanges are treated like investments—they earn interest. The giver will receive the principal plus interest in the form of a bigger, better gift from the recipient the next time there is a meeting.

For this reason, it is advisable to keep the gifts more symbolic than expensive. An executive of a manufacturing company, for example, can give samples of his company products or items representative of his home region. A trade delegation from the state of Oklahoma, for instance, gave state flags with certificates, noting that the flags had been flown over their state capitol.

The more personal the gift, the better. If you have shared an experience with the recipient, such as a golf game, give something to commemorate that event. Golf equipment, framed photographs or inscribed books about a related topic make great gifts that remind your counterpart of the shared experience. I once had an agent in Taiwan who loved a certain series of mystery books. Each time I visited him, I would bring along the latest book in the series for him. If you know what your acquaintance's hobbies are or those of his or her family members, try to give gifts related to those hobbies. Most Taiwanese children like T-shirts and caps with printed cartoon characters or school logos.

It is quite acceptable to give a gift with your company logo on it as long as the logo is not too conspicuous. A conspicuous display of the logo is not only in bad taste but can be viewed as self-glorifying. Boasting of one's company's achievements is, to the Taiwanese, as boorish as touting one's own accomplishments.

I recommend selecting gifts that mean something to you, such as souvenirs from your country or region. If you come from the state of Oklahoma in the United States, for example, the Indian (native American) craftwork indigenous to the region makes a unique gift. Malaysians might want to give something made from the excellent pewter their crafts people are famous for.

The Taiwanese also give presents that can be consumed, such as cooking oil and other selected foods. If you represent a food company, this is a perfect opportunity to present your product as a gift. Be sure the presentation (packaging) is first class. Gourmet gifts have a special cachet. Such gifts include soups, coffee, estate wines, foreign candies and designer items.

Have gifts properly wrapped. A neat and attractive presentation is noted and appreciated. Sloppy overuse of wrapping tape is undesirable. Gold and red are "lucky" colours. Avoid black or white paper. It is difficult, if not impossible, to wrap your gifts at home and fly halfway around the world with them and arrive with the gifts in good condition. If the contents are not broken, the wrapping will likely be dented and wrinkled by the wear and tear of travel. Have your gifts wrapped by the hotel gift shop. Not only will the customer service assistants be knowledgeable about appropriate packaging but you will have "fresh-looking gifts" to present.

Chapter 8

Business Culture and Communications

The Taiwanese Business Person
"The Taiwanese don't know what they want, but they're ready to bite somebody to get it."

—Anonymous

Actually, the Taiwanese business person does know what he or she wants, and this is business. And he or she knows exactly how to get it. A common mistake foreign business people make in Taiwan is assuming that the Taiwanese need to be taught how to do business. The Taiwanese can, and have, taught the world what business is. How else can one explain this small island's (21.4 million people or 0.4% of the world's population) ranking of 11 in the world in import value and 18 in exports as of 1998?

The Taiwanese understand business almost as well as they appreciate fine cooking. Their approach to business is as unique as is their approach to cooking. To understand this approach, you must first understand their culture. Their language, value system, sense of taste and style of communication are unique and profoundly affect the way they conduct business. Any discussion of Taiwanese business culture should begin with the Chinese/Taiwanese concept of *guanxi*.

Guanxi

Guanxi or "kwanshi" as it is often romanised in Taiwan, is the concept of relationship networking. The Taiwanese version of networking goes beyond what most non-Chinese perceive as networking. There are two components to guanxi—knowing people and exchanging favours with them. Anyone doing business in Taiwan must learn and practice guanxi or be left out in the cold.

The key to succeeding at the guanxi game is to expand your network of Taiwanese contacts and to cultivate relationships simultaneously. Cultivating relationships means doing favours for your acquaintances and keeping them in mind—that is, not forgetting to send them new year greeting cards, not forgetting the favours they do for you and most definitely, not forgetting them when you can toss some business their way. However, this only works if you honestly have your friends' best interests at heart. Being usury or manipulative does nothing to improve one's life.

Obligations

In the process of doing favours for one another, indebtedness is created. The Taiwanese norm of reciprocity requires that these social debts be honoured when one is called on to do so. Within Taiwanese culture, this *quid pro quo* is taken seriously. One who does not return a favour is out of favour.

A unique aspect of the Taiwanese quid pro quo concept is its application across longer expanses of time than is common in most cultures. Even the son or daughter can be held accountable for obligations incurred by a parent. It is also possible for an obligation to be repaid indirectly to a third party. If executive A owes executive B a favour, for example, it is not out of the ordinary for executive B to ask executive A to do a favour for executive C, someone executive B owes a favour to. In Taiwan, favours and obligations function as a social currency that can be transferred from one person to another.

Relating to Your Taiwanese Counterparts

The foreign business person should keep in mind that the Taiwanese interact with one another on only one level—the personal level. Individuals in many other cultures, especially

Western cultures, interact on two levels—personal and professional. Business people in Western cultures can disagree vehemently with one another over a task-oriented business issue but get along very well on a personal level. The Taiwanese tend to take matters personally both in business and personal relations. It is difficult to argue with a Taiwanese business partner and still maintain a good personal relationship with him or her.

Remember that to most Taiwanese business people, the personal relationship comes before product attributes (price, novelty, etc.) and legal restraints in their decision-making process. In deciding which foreign company to do business with, a Taiwanese business person will often opt to buy from company A if they show respect for his/her dignity, even if company B's product is cheaper and/or better. The order of priority of matters differs for Taiwanese and Westerners.

What Comes First

Taiwanese

First priority:	Relationship
Second priority:	Product attributes
Third priority:	Legal

Westerners

First priority:	Product attributes
Second priority:	Legal
Third priority:	Relationship

I know of at least one case where a perceived slight cost a US company a multi-million dollar deal with a Taiwanese buyer of industrial machinery. The owner of the medium-sized Taiwanese corporation visited two potential suppliers of the type of equipment his company needed. One of the equipment makers was a German company, the other a US company. When he visited the German company, the Germans entertained him for two days with a tightly packed itinerary that left no time for relaxation. When the Taiwanese executive visited the US supplier, he found that the Americans had left half a day in the schedule open and unplanned.

The president of the US company had travelled internationally on business many times and had often chaffed at his Taiwanese hosts who had planned every waking moment for him. He had often wished that his hosts would give him some time to explore on his own. When planning the itinerary for the visiting Taiwanese, the American had therefore left time for his guest to explore on his own. Unfortunately, the Taiwanese executive did not perceive this as the thoughtful gesture it was supposed to be. The Taiwanese perceived the time he was left alone as an indication that the Americans did not respect him enough to spend time with him. He gave his business to the Germans.

It is, therefore, essential to not only show respect for your Taiwanese counterpart but to also take pains to understand his or her values and how he or she may interpret or misinterpret your actions. The crucial step in the process of reacting to another's behaviour is how we interpret the behaviour of the other person. As we have seen in the example of the US company above, well-intended behaviour can be completely misinterpreted.

A High Context Culture

Taiwan is what sociologists call a "high context" culture. Members of such cultures attach more importance to *the way* a message is communicated than the content of the message—relative to low context cultures such as North America and Europe. To the Taiwanese, "getting in sync" with each other is a prerequisite for an exchange to succeed. What this means to foreign business people from low context cultures is that consummating a business deal may take longer than expected and it may not happen at all if they do not put effort into building the relationship first.

However, Taiwanese business people engage in less preliminary relationship-building than do their cousins on the mainland or the Japanese. The Taiwanese devotion to the short-term return-on-investment and the "bottom line" cuts through some of the relationship-building obligation. In this respect, the Taiwanese lie somewhere between the Japanese and the Americans on the "I've got to like you before I do business with you" continuum.

The Language

English and Japanese are understood by many Taiwanese. English is widely spoken in business and government circles. Those Taiwanese educated prior to 1945 during the Japanese colonial period often speak Japanese.

There are several Chinese languages and dozens of Chinese dialects, but Mandarin is dominant. Originally spoken in the Beijing area of northern China, Mandarin has been promoted by both the mainland Chinese and Taiwan-based Nationalist government as the national language. Mandarin, or *guo yu* (national language) is taught in schools from Hong Kong to Beijing to Taipei and is widely spoken and understood by the Chinese everywhere.

The Taiwanese Language

While Mandarin is taught in schools throughout the PRC and in Taiwan, the people still speak their native tongue as their first language. Over 50% of the Taiwan population speak Taiwanese, a Chinese dialect known as Hakka. Within the Taiwanese community, the Taiwanese dialect is often used for business. When speaking to non-Taiwanese Chinese, the Taiwanese usually use Mandarin. Virtually all Taiwanese speak and understand Mandarin, especially if they had received their education after 1949.

The refugees of the war with the communists, who fled to Taiwan, brought their various native Chinese tongues with them. Cantonese, Shanghainese, Hakka, Mandarin and many other

Chinese languages and dialects can be heard on the streets of Taiwan today.

Chinese Characters

While the Chinese have several mutually unintelligible spoken languages, they can all read the written language. The core group of Chinese developed a written language of symbols or ideograms before they dispersed and developed different spoken languages. Since the ideograms were pictures of things or concepts and not a phonetic alphabet, the Chinese could continue to use the same symbol to represent an object but pronounce it differently.

Learning Taiwanese

If you plan to be in Taiwan for the long haul or to travel there frequently, it would be a good idea to study Mandarin or Taiwanese. If you can learn to do no more than carry on a polite conversation in either language, you will increase your chances of success in business and society exponentially. The Taiwanese appreciate efforts by foreigners to learn their language and see it as a gesture of goodwill.

Some Essential Expressions

Mandarin is not an easy language to learn, but millions of foreigners have managed to learn it. Much of the difficulty lies in the tonality of the language. Each syllable in Mandarin can have four different tones—level tone, rising tone, dropping tone and dipping tone—each with its own meaning. For example, the one syllable *ma* can mean "mother", "horse", "scold" or "hemp", depending on the tone with which it is said.

Here are a few Chinese phrases worth learning:

Speak Mandarin

English	Mandarin	Pronunciation
thank you	xie xie ni	shieh shieh nee
hello	ni hao ma	nee how ma
goodbye	zai jian	jai jien
excuse me	dui bu qi	dway boo chee
How much does	Shi duo shao	Shi dwo shao
this cost?	qian?	chien
please	qing	ching
today	jin tian	jeen tyen
tomorrow	ming tian	ming tyen
yesterday	zuo tian	dzaw tyen

Verbal Communication

The Concept of "Face"

Achieving and maintaining a positive sense of self is important to everyone. This is *very* important to the Taiwanese. "Face" or *mian zi*, is roughly equivalent to respect or prestige. If one has wealth, intelligence, dignity, position or attractiveness, one is said to "have face". If one is embarrassed or shamed, one "loses face"—no one likes to "lose face".

The key to building positive business relationships with the Taiwanese is to "give face" and avoid causing a "loss of face". This is best accomplished by understanding the culture in its myriad aspects (see the section on "Taboos" below).

While the "saving" and "loss of face" is very important between Taiwanese, it is less important between Taiwanese and foreigners. After all, foreigners are given some benefit of the doubt due to their ignorance of the culture. "How can I hold the foreigner responsible for causing me a loss of face?", a Taiwanese might say, "He's foreign!" However, this magnanimity only goes so far.

Be wary of making business decisions based on advice from Taiwan executives that it is critical to their "face", which is often used as a business tactic by Taiwanese executives. To gain leverage with their foreign business counterparts, some Taiwanese will allege that unless they get their way, they will suffer a "loss of face". I know of one case where a Taiwanese purchasing manager told a British salesman that unless he sold the product in question to him at a certain low rate, he would "lose face" with his Taiwanese boss and be shamed. The appeal to the British salesman's sympathy actually worked in this case.

Harmony
The Confucian devotion to harmony in human relations is the basis for life in Taiwan. The Taiwanese are concerned with the proper treatment of one another and desirous of avoiding hurt to other people's feelings.

Frankness
You should avoid speaking too frankly. The Taiwanese say what they think their friends would like to hear—to "preserve" one another's "face". Beating about the bush or being circumspect is a basic communication skill in Taiwan.

Delivering Criticism
Humiliating someone, especially a co-worker or subordinate, in public is considered boorish behaviour and harms the reputation of the one who humiliates more than that of the person being criticised. Causing a "loss of face" to another will earn the perpetrator disdain. If criticism must be delivered, do it in the privacy of your room with the person involved and with tact.

It is also considered poor conduct to publicly criticise your competition or their representatives. Sell your product or service attributes, but do not denigrate your competition directly. If a direct comparison of product or service is needed, it is best to bury a comparative chart in your sales materials so that you make your point with some subtlety. Direct comparative advertising is still rare in Taiwan.

How to Disagree
In every culture, people have to take positions and find ways to express disagreement. This must be dealt with in a way that guarantees some degree of efficiency and cooperation. So how do you express disagreement in a culture that cherishes harmony and tries to avoid "loss of face"?

In situations where you find yourself disagreeing with superiors within your own organisation or with senior members of another organisation, keep in mind the Confucian ideal to honour the hierarchy. In disagreeing with a superior, the key is to accord him or her "face". This is best done by first discussing the good points of his or her idea or view and then carefully suggesting an alternative that could "build upon" the good idea. If at all possible, do this in private—in a one-on-one discussion with the person you are disagreeing with.

If a face-to-face disagreement is unavoidable, use vague language that is gradually clarified until the other side gets the message—hopefully without being offended. If all else fails, do not hesitate to frankly state your position. While some toes may be stepped on, this is preferable to a gross misunderstanding.

Sensitive Topics of Conversation
Every culture has its "in-bounds" and "out-of-bounds" behaviours and topics of discussion. What is acceptable as a topic of conversation in one culture is completely unacceptable in another. It should therefore come as no surprise that what passes as normal questioning in Taiwan can be offensive to some foreigners. Likewise, what some foreigners consider to be "friendly" topics can, to the Taiwanese, seem inappropriate.

In some cultures, it is acceptable to speak freely about emotions and feelings, but the Taiwanese prefer reserve. Even those you feel you have grown close to can be embarrassed by discussions of a personal or intimate nature. While it may seem obvious that discussions of a very personal nature should be off limits, what may seem personal to you may not be considered so by others, and vice versa. For example, among the Taiwanese and Chinese, it is not considered improper to ask another why he or she has no children. In other cultures, such as the United States, such a question is considered taboo.

In some Western cultures, personal privacy is prized and defended aggressively—everyone is supposed to mind his or her own affairs. However, in Taiwan, taking an interest in certain aspects of another person's life can signal your care for him or her. The key words here are "certain aspects". When your Taiwanese friend tells you, "You have put on weight", don't get upset. He or she is just trying to be friendly, even complimentary. In Taiwan, a person's weight is not the sensitive, personal topic it is in the West. Portliness has long been a sign of wealth in Chinese society and only in recent years has it become negative, as the health effects of obesity become understood.

Family is another topic open to inquiry in Taiwan. The Taiwanese are particularly interested in families and a question such as, "When are you going to get married?" is common. Questions about financial matters are also common. "How much do you make?" or "How much rent do you pay?" are also common questions that seem to be acceptable in the Taiwanese society. However, to many foreigners, these questions seem intrusive and even rude.

In Taiwan, political opinions can be considered personal and questioning in this area can make others uncomfortable. If your Taiwanese friends do reveal such matters to you, never break their trust by telling others about the matter.

The best way to deal with uncomfortable questions is to deflect them in a good-natured manner. Rather than snap at your Taiwanese acquaintance, give him or her a vague or humorous answer. If asked what your salary is, you might simply reply, "I'm not yet a millionaire" or "It's hard to say" instead of "It's none of your business!" Do not hesitate to turn the tables and ask your interrogator the same questions.

Taiwanese business people are equally inquisitive about their business partner's financial status. Questions about profits and costs are not uncommon. Most foreign business people consider such matters proprietary and do not wish to reveal them. The Taiwanese generally consider such matters corporate secrets as well but figure that they can "get away" with asking such questions—assuming their foreign partner will dismiss the impropriety as simply a difference in culture. Of course, this can go both ways. Foreign business people can and do try to use cultural misunderstanding as a licence to do things they would not normally do within their own cultures.

Do not give away any information you would not at home. Assume that any information you do give away, even to government agencies, will be known by third parties. One US manufacturer of medical equipment was chagrined to find that manufacturing cost and process information it gave to a Taiwanese company was later given to its primary competitor in the United States when the Taiwan company began doing business with that competitor. The US company had become lax in its security precautions because it felt that the Taiwanese company was far from its primary market and had little to lose. Big mistake. The Taiwanese company used the information from the first US company to negotiate from a position of strength with the second US company.

Taboos

The following constitute some common taboos in Taiwanese culture that foreign business people should steer clear of:

- Do not use red ink to write letters or notes. It is acceptable for a teacher to correct homework with a red pen, but a significant amount of writing in red should be avoided.
- Clocks should not be chosen as gifts for the Taiwanese. The Mandarin word for "clock" sounds similar to that for "termination" that has an implication of death. Therefore, giving people clocks can be considered to bring them bad luck.
- Umbrellas are not good gifts for lovers. In Mandarin, "umbrella" sounds similar to "separation", which denotes a break-up.
- The seventh lunar month, which normally falls around July or August in the Gregorian calendar, is considered the ghost month, when the Chinese believe spirits of the dead roam the Earth. The Taiwanese avoid many activities during this period. They believe that such activities as weddings, moving house, travelling and non-emergency medical operations should be avoided during this month. Mischievous or hostile ghosts may interfere with the important matters of the living during the ghost month.
- Superstitious Taiwanese believe that if you say something will happen, it will happen. For instance, they believe that if you say, "Watch out for the knife or you will hurt yourself", it will increase the chances of your friend actually hurting himself/ herself. Such statements should be avoided, especially during the Lunar New Year holidays, when the trend for the coming year is believed to be set (or created) by what one does on that day.
- In Taiwan, the colour white is related to death. It is acceptable to dress in white for ordinary affairs such as work or school but it is considered inappropriate for occasions like a wedding banquet (the bride and the bridegroom are obvious exceptions in the western-style wedding banquets).

An Aversion to Talking to Strangers

The Taiwanese have a saying, "First time strangers, second time friends". The Taiwanese are generally friendly, but they do not readily strike up conversations with strangers. To Australians and Americans, initiating a conversation with strangers is one way of getting to know new people and to expand their network of contacts. The Taiwanese, on the other hand, make a distinction between acquaintances and strangers. They see no need to talk to strangers as their needs are either fulfilled within the realm of their existing circle of acquaintances or they rely on known intermediaries to help them expand their circle.

The Intermediary

The role of the intermediary is very important in the Taiwanese culture. The intermediary expands social circles by bridging the gap between members of the circle. Every society has these "matchmakers", but none excel at it the way the Chinese do and none place more responsibility on the shoulders of the intermediary or introducer. By introducing mutual acquaintances, he or she takes on the responsibility for the future relationship between the two. If one of the people he or she introduces treats the other one badly, he or she is expected to try to make right the wrong.

For this reason, you should be careful when acting as an intermediary in Taiwan. Think carefully before introducing two of your business acquaintances to each other. If the relationship sours, you may receive some of the blame. Do not act as a go-between for businesses or people you are not comfortable with or whose reputation you cannot vouch for.

Deflecting Compliments

It is considered poor manners to readily accept compliments. The Taiwanese enjoy compliments but to simply say "Thank you" in response to a compliment is considered arrogance. Humility is a much-valued trait among the Taiwanese, while boastfulness and conceit are disdained. To show the proper humility, the right response to the above compliment would be "Oh no, not at all!" or *"nali nali"* in Mandarin.

In business situations such as a job interview or performance review, keep this humility trait in mind. Do not expect your employees or interviewees to aggressively tout their skills and experience. Do not take them at their self-effacing word and dismiss them as untalented! For the foreign executive, it is equally important to avoid boasting about your own accomplishments or those of your company's. Let third parties do the "dirty work" for you.

Never underestimate the importance of the third party in the Taiwanese society. Be ready and willing to perform the role of the third party complimentor or introducer yourself. Since the recipient of compliments cannot properly accept the accolade, it is essential that the "neutral" third party step in to second the compliment. The one who benefits is expected to return the favour in the future.

Tone of Voice

While they do not always practise it, the Taiwanese appreciate a moderate voice. In speaking with your Taiwanese counterparts, use a volume that is loud enough to be easily heard but not loud enough to be aggressive. People all over the world seem to think that the louder they speak to foreigners, the better they will understand—even if they do not understand the language being directed at them. If you speak too loudly to your Taiwanese counterparts, they will be embarrassed because they are concerned that others will think they are being criticised publicly. Their "loss of face" will result in a disinclination to communicate at all.

Non-verbal Communication

Dress

The key to dressing for success in Taiwan is to dress conservatively. No cutting-edge fashion, bright colours or revealing clothing in the workplace.

Male executives wear Western-style suits and ties. When the weather is particularly hot, the men dispense with the suit jacket whenever possible. Do as your Taiwanese counterpart does. If he appears without a jacket or even a tie, feel free to remove yours.

Female executives wear businesslike dresses, pant suits or skirt and jacket combinations. As with men, the ladies' dress is conservative. Hemlines are not far above the knee and colours are subdued.

Body Language

Here are some tips for avoiding misunderstandings:

- Do not summon others by wagging your index finger. Only animals or people one despises are called this way. The Taiwanese summon others by waving the four fingers back and forth with the palm turned down.
- When handing an object to others, it is polite to hand it to them with both hands.
- Do not touch, back-slap, or point. Physical contact, except shaking hands, should be avoided.
- No fist pounding on tables or raised voices to emphasise points. Self-control is respected. Visible anger causes a loss of respect.
- The Taiwanese do not bow to each other—but they do nod their heads when greeting and shaking hands.

Business Entertaining

The Taiwanese are hospitable people. While they can do business without building a relationship, they do not. They like people and enjoy showing them a good time. Business entertaining is a manifestation of this outlook on life. Be prepared to entertain and be entertained.

It starts innocently enough with an invitation to lunch or dinner. Before you know it, you are singing "Blue Suede Shoes" before a small crowd at a karaoke bar and downing small goblets of Chinese sorghum wine.

If you are in Taiwan on business and contacting businesses directly to set up meetings, feel free to invite your Taiwanese counterparts to lunch if you are having a late morning meeting. Reserve late-morning meeting slots for those contacts you particularly want to get to know. Inviting your key contacts to lunch is one of the best ways to get to know them and to jump-start a business relationship. If you are unfamiliar with Taiwan and the eateries near where you will be meeting them prior to lunch, either invite them to lunch in a hotel or ask them for a recommendation.

After getting to know your Taiwanese business partners, feel free to invite them to dinner. Selecting the right restaurant and cuisine is important to making the evening a success. If you live in Taiwan or travel there frequently, establish your patronage at a few good restaurants as a regular customer. The special treatment you receive and recognition by the restaurant staff will enhance the impression you make on your guests. The quickest way to establish such a restaurant-valued customer relationship is to ask your established Taiwan contacts to introduce you to their favourite restaurant. Network your way into the Taiwanese fine restaurant scene.

If you belong to a private club at home, check to see if they have affiliate clubs in Taiwan. If they do, try them out and see if they will be suitable for your future guests. The exclusive

---

Gan Bei!

The Taiwanese like to drink together, especially to form bonds with those they do business with. I am not much of a drinker and was unprepared for the sheer quantity of Maotai (a potent Chinese sorghum spirit) and beer that the Taiwanese drink at banquets and dinners. The president of one large conglomerate, a man in his 80s, went around the table challenging every one of us to *"gan bei"* (literally "dry cup"), or down the contents of glasses. He must have downed at least 12 glasses to each of our one, but he was still going strong when we left. It seemed to me the further south we went in Taiwan, the more they drank at banquets. In Kaohsiung, our Taiwanese friends had us drinking wine from bowls and we were rather drunk within an hour. They love to challenge you and demonstrate their drinking ability. This is a tough place for non-drinkers.

— A business person from Santa Barbara, USA

---

nature of most of these private clubs may add to their allure for your guests.

A willingness to dine Taiwanese-style will make a good impression on your Taiwanese guests. Do not take them to a Western-style restaurant unless you know they like the cuisine. The safest way to start off is to invite your guests to a fine Taiwanese restaurant the first time and in the course of the dinner, inquire about their favourite foreign cuisines. Note their comments for future references.

Another "safe" alternative is to invite your guests to one of the many excellent buffet-style restaurants in Taiwan's major hotels, such as the Grand Formosa Regent and the Grand Hyatt in Taipei. Many of these restaurants offer an international buffet spread, which includes Taiwanese, Japanese and Western dishes. Many of these restaurants also have private dining rooms that you can reserve.

Dinner Conversation

Dinner is a social event and not the time to discuss business unless your counterpart brings it up. Talk about general topics of common interest over dinner. Find out the likes and dislikes of your partners—sports, travel destinations, hobbies, music, etc. Get to know your partners' out-of-office lives. Serious conversation sometimes comes after dinner over drinks.

Avoid controversial topics with the potential to spoil the mood. Avoid politics and religion.

Unless all the participants are fluent in English, there may be times when the Taiwanese participants speak among themselves in Chinese. Unless they do this all evening to your exclusion, do not be offended. "Shop talk" about matters within one's organisation is the most likely reason.

Drinking

It is common among the Taiwanese to get together for a drink after work. This is simply a way of socialising and developing a sense of trust among people. In Taiwan, drinking and singing together are the most common ways for people to develop strong relationships. One middle-aged section chief explained that these activities provide access to the real person behind the public face that everyone is expected to wear—"Getting slightly drunk or singing in public are somewhat embarrassing situations that break down barriers between people that share them."

Karaoke or KTV

This unique style of entertainment originated in Japan (*karaoke* means "empty orchestra" in Japanese) but has flourished in Taiwan. Often called "KTV" in Taiwan, the venue is a club with private rooms available to small groups of people who come to drink and sing along to music videos. The words to the songs appear on the video screen so the singer, microphone in hand, can sing along with the music. The rooms are comfortably furnished with a central coffee table surrounded by sofas and plush chairs.

Groups of four to eight people will reserve a private room for anywhere from two to several hours of partying. Participants enjoy drinks and side dishes of peanuts and rice crackers while getting to know each other between songs. This is particularly popular with college students and co-workers. Executives frequent posh, expensive karaoke clubs that cater specially to them, some of which are private clubs with attractive hostesses to keep the businessmen company. The hostesses pour drinks, engage in small talk, joke and generally work to keep spirits up. They are not expected to engage in any sexual behaviour. The host for the evening will tip the hostesses at the end of the evening.

When the drinks arrive, the basic rule is that no one pours his or her own drink. If a hostess is not there to pour the drinks, you should do so for those sitting next to you or let them pour your drink for you. When pouring the drink, it is polite to use both hands or to support the hand that is holding the bottle with the other hand. Hold your glass up with both hands as the other person pours your drink.

A night of partying at an executive-style karaoke club can be jaw-dropping expensive. It is not uncommon for the bill to total several hundred US dollars or even more. Before inviting your guests to such an event, be prepared for the expense.

Footing the Bill

Remember that the person who issues the invitation is expected to pay for everyone. "Going Dutch" and splitting the bill among participants is unheard of in the Taiwanese business circles. At the end of a meal or evening of entertainment, your guests may try to pay the bill as a polite gesture. Do not let them. If you invited them, you must settle the bill. To impress your guests, arrange to take care of the bill in advance or after the guests have left so no bill appears while they are there. You may have a subordinate leave the table discreetly to pay the bill before it is brought out.

Other Types of Entertainment

Drinking and singing are not the only activities that will create a bond with business partners. Golf, baseball and basketball are popular sports in Taiwan and offer great opportunities for spending time with those you want to know better.

Basketball Hoops is big in Taiwan. The Chinese Basketball Alliance (CBA), a professional league, began November-to-June seasons in 1996. Six corporate-owned teams do battle in 13 cities around the island over the eight-month long season. The Hung Fu Rams, Hung Kuo Elephants, Chungshing Tigers, Yulon Dinos, Tera Mars and the Luckipar of the CBA are not associated with any one city so they draw fans from all across the island.

It is not difficult to catch a game if you are in Taiwan during the season. Over 150 regular season games are played and tickets are usually available. Expect the games to be noisy, flashy and crowded. Most of the basketball fans are young girls and most arenas are small, seating 2,700 to 4,500 fans. If you want to attend a sports event, your hotel concierge should be able to arrange tickets for you.

Negotiating Taiwanese-style

The Taiwanese have a reputation for being tough negotiators. Business people here are aggressive, persistent and willing to exploit any weakness or opening. The success of any business venture in Taiwan is directly related to the outcome of negotiations with business representatives and government officials. In order to negotiate successfully in Taiwan, foreign companies should be sensitive to Taiwanese values, behavioural patterns and psychology, as well as business matters. The following is a list of points the Australian Business Centre recommends that companies doing

business in Taiwan consider, including tactics they should expect
to encounter during negotiations with the Taiwanese:

- Good preparation is essential to achieving an acceptable result.
  Expect the Taiwanese to know your company, your products
  and the industry, and to ask penetrating questions. Foreign
  companies that are new to the market are often surprised at the
  detailed questions asked by their Taiwanese counterparts. Ensure
  that you have all the relevant information at hand.
- Investigate the Taiwanese company's business markets, financial
  status and reputation prior to your first meeting. Research current
  economic conditions and government policies in Taiwan as
  thoroughly as possible.
- In most negotiating sessions, the Taiwanese will speak both
  Chinese (Mandarin or Taiwanese) and English. This is often
  advantageous for the Taiwanese since they can discuss a matter
  without leaving the room. Foreign negotiators should have a
  Chinese-speaking member on their team. Feel free to excuse
  yourself to discuss points of negotiation in private.
- Do not feel compelled to fill in silences that occur during
  negotiations. Westerners are particularly uncomfortable with
  such silences and typically make statements to fill what they
  feel to be an awkward period, even to the extent of making
  unnecessary concessions. Staying silent is particularly useful if
  the Taiwanese have made an unreasonable demand or proposal.
  If you refuse to give in to the "silent treatment" and show that
  you will not be rattled into making concessions, your Taiwanese
  counterpart will likely proceed with negotiations in the hope
  of finding a mutually acceptable solution.
- The pace of the negotiations will inevitably be slower than
  expected. The conversation at the beginning of a meeting is
  often informal and not related to business. The Taiwanese believe
  it is important to establish a relationship and will focus their
  efforts on learning about the negotiators and their company

before concentrating on the agreement. It is unreasonable to expect business decisions to be made during an initial meeting. If you must have an immediate response, always send a written proposal well before the meeting.

- In general, agreements should be short, easy to understand and broadly phrased. Time spent haggling over small details is often counterproductive.
- It is vital to have proper legal advice in negotiations with Taiwanese companies, particularly where intellectual property issues are involved. Bear in mind that the law in Taiwan is different from most other countries.
- It is often preferable to have your attorney operate behind the scene rather than across the negotiating table. The presence of attorneys often intimidates the Taiwanese business person, who has a less legalistic approach to contracts and business relationships. Most Taiwanese companies have their legal representatives check any contract or agreement before signing it.
- The Taiwanese are sensitive to the atmosphere of the negotiation. They will react unfavourably to a person they consider to be impolite, harsh or arrogant, and appreciate someone who is sincere, polite and persistent.
- Negotiations always continue after the agreement is signed. In fact, the really important negotiations take place as the venture progresses. The real substance of the relationship develops as the two parties negotiate day-to-day issues and events. For substantial investments, on-the-ground representation in Taiwan is particularly crucial to the success of the business venture.
- The Taiwanese believe that the relationship between the relevant parties should prevent any conflict or dispute from arising. If parties are forced to resort to formal legal process to resolve a dispute, a public admission has been made that the relationship has failed. As a result, if a dispute becomes public knowledge, both parties will be considered to be at fault, regardless of the

merit of any one party's position. This aversion to litigation is due in part to a different perception of an individual's rights and the tradition of delegating the resolution of disputes to non-official mechanisms.

- The saying, "Your floor is our ceiling", is often heard from Taiwanese buyers towards the end of a long discussion on price. It simply means that the lowest price you are offering to sell at is the maximum price they would even consider.

- A traditional view of contracts as instruments that must change with changing circumstances is still widely accepted among the Taiwanese. If the business climate changes substantially from the time of signing the contract, the Taiwanese will often insist on re-negotiating the contract to fit current circumstances.

Food

Professionals travelling in Taiwan can expect to find themselves at the ubiquitous banquet. Some enjoy the experience, others dread it. Most start out enjoying them and soon end up hating them. The Taiwanese do not help matters—they seem to be obsessed with eating.

It is a truism that Taiwanese travelling abroad will go to great lengths to get their hosts to take them to a Chinese restaurant. On the other hand, the foreigner travelling in Taiwan will rarely be blessed with a dinner featuring his or her familiar home cuisine.

Taiwan is a microcosm of Chinese cuisine. People from all over China found their way to Taiwan and brought their food styles with them. There are dozens of Chinese cuisines commonly available in Taiwan but four dominate: the northern or Mandarin style of Beijing, the southern or Cantonese style, the Shanghai style and the western or Szechuan style.

It is not uncommon for Taiwanese restaurants to have over three hundred items on their menus. The choices can be mind boggling. In most business situations however, the foreign guest need not worry as the host or the restaurant selects the dishes for everyone. The dishes are communal.

Those on special diets (including vegetarians) should appraise their hosts of this well before a dinner or banquet. In most cases, the host will arrange for a special meal to be served to the person/s needing the special meal.

Dining Etiquette

Most dining tables are round and seat about four to twelve guests. There is usually a large turntable or "Lazy Susan" in the centre of the table on which the serving platters are placed. In most cases, in front of each diner will be placed a rice bowl, a pair of chopsticks on a chopstick rest to the right, a soup bowl with a porcelain soup spoon, a small flat plate, and to the right a small dish for soy sauce or chilli sauce. A teacup or a glass will be placed at the top of each setting.

During most formal dinners and banquets, the dishes are served in courses. The serving dishes are placed on the turntable and shared among the diners. People serve themselves using the common serving spoons or large serving chopsticks on the turntable. Feel free to help yourself to second helpings from the serving dishes.

Chinese tea is poured into handle-less cups from a teapot on the table. Chinese tea is drunk without milk or sugar. Hold your cup with your thumb and index finger on opposite sides of the top rim and with your small finger supporting the base of the cup. Using both hands to lift the cup to your mouth is courteous. If you do not want anymore tea, either leave the cup full or just hold your hand over the cup when more tea is offered.

Chinese Rice Wine

Chinese wine or *jiu* is made from rice or sorghum and is served during most banquets and dinners. *Bai jiu*, or white wine, is a common sorghum-based spirit. Chinese wine is usually served warm with meals.

Toasting

At Taiwanese dinners or banquets with a guest-of-honour present, it is customary for the host to offer a toast to him or her before the meal begins. The host raises his cup in a toast and takes a sip of his drink, followed by all the guests. The host then picks up his chopsticks or utensils, gestures towards the food and invites everyone to eat. After being invited to do so, the guest-of-honour serves himself first. Then the other guests help themselves to the communal serving dishes. The host serves himself last.

The Taiwanese love to toast to the health and happiness of others and dinners are punctuated with frequent toasting. Any drink, whether alcohol, tea or soft drinks, can be used for toasting. Hold the cup or glass in both hands about chest high, look at the person being toasted and say *"Gan bei"* or "Cheers". Then, drink from your cup and raise it in the direction of the person being toasted while dipping your head in a symbolic bow before placing your cup back on the table.

Rice

At some very formal meals, the rice is served near the end of the courses. At other meals, the rice is served in a communal bowl that guests help themselves from. Use the serving spoon to scoop rice out of the serving bowl into your own rice bowl. Eat rice directly from your own bowl using chopsticks. Pick your rice bowl up with one hand with your four fingers under the bowl and your thumb resting on the top rim to steady the bowl. Hold the bowl at chin level and rest the rim on your lower lip. Move (or shovel) the rice into your mouth using chopsticks. Watch how your fellow diners accomplish this feat.

Noodles

Only the Italians take noodles more seriously than the Taiwanese. Noodles have long been an important staple for the Chinese. In

Taiwan, it is common to have noodles daily. And quite often, they are even considered to be a complete meal.

There are many varieties of noodles. The most common types are made from wheat, rice or bean flour. Noodles also play a role as the traditional Chinese symbol of longevity, the length of the noodles symbolising the length of life.

Chopsticks and Toothpicks

The key to using chopsticks is practice. If you do not know how to use them yet, buy a pair of chopsticks and practise using them at home. Here are some tips on their proper use:

- Hold the chopsticks two-thirds up its length (near the thicker end).
- Tap the eating (thin) ends on the table to make them level.
- Wedge one stick into the base of the thumb and index finger. Let it rest on the tip of the ring finger.
- Hold the other stick on top of the other one as you would a pencil.
- The top chopstick does the work, moving up and down in a pincer-like movement against the stationary stick at the bottom.

During rites to honour a family's ancestors, chopsticks are placed upright in a bowl of steamed rice. This gesture is meant to symbolise the family's concern for the nourishment and wellbeing of the ancestors. It is therefore considered to be in poor taste to leave one's chopsticks resting upright in a bowl of rice at the dining table. Chopsticks, when not in use, should be placed on the chopstick rest. Other things considered taboo in regard to using chopsticks in polite company include the following:

- Do not suck on your chopsticks.
- Do not point or gesticulate with them.
- Do not cross one over the other when you set them down.

Toothpicks are usually made available at the end of a Taiwanese meal. Cup one hand over your mouth as you use the toothpick with the other hand.

Living On Taiwan Time

Anyone familiar with the Chinese societies of Taiwan, Singapore (largely Chinese), Hong Kong and mainland China knows that there are dramatic differences in the pace of life in general, and certainly of life in the business realm. Hong Kong has the fastest pace—more so than Japan. Mainland China has the slowest pace. Taiwan is somewhere in between.

For example, the walking pace of the people, the time it takes for financial transactions, etc. is faster in Taiwan than on the mainland but slower than in Hong Kong. The effort put into keeping schedules and maintaining the accuracy of clocks is greater in Singapore and Hong Kong than in Taiwan. Trains in Taiwan do not always run on time—they do in Singapore. Trains never run on time in mainland China.

The Taiwanese try to do many things at once rather than doing one thing at a time, as the Northern Europeans and Americans do. They tend to put more importance on the completion of a matter and the people involved than on the strict adherence to predetermined schedules. The Taiwanese also take a longer term view of matters than do most other cultures. They tend to feel comfortable with very long-range plans and they often wait patiently for an outcome they desire. It is as if their long history of several thousand years has accustomed them to take a historical and cyclic view of events and to cultivate patience.

When it comes to Return on Investment (ROI), however, the Chinese entrepreneurs of Taiwan can be very impatient to reach profit status. The Chinese of Taiwan were some of the first to invest in hotel properties in communist Vietnam—but they structured the deals to assure a very rapid ROI that would achieve break-even status quickly, often within three years of opening.

The Chinese of Taiwan are generally polite but frank. The Taiwanese prefer the straightforward approach to life and respect those who communicate diplomatically but honestly. To the Taiwanese business person, the bottom-line is what counts most.

Basic Facts and Travel Tips

Airports

Taiwan has two international airports. Chiang Kai Shek International Airport (known as "CKS") serves Taipei, while Kaohsiung International Airport serves the southern port city of Kaohsiung. CKS is located near Taoyuan, 40 km west of Taipei or about 45 minutes to an hour from most hotels in the city. Kaohsiung International is in the city. The taxi fare ranges from NT$300–400 within Kaohsiung.

The departure tax from Taiwan is NT$300. Some hotels sell the departure tax ticket upon check-out so you do not have to be hassled with it at the airport.

If you stop in Taiwan for 72 hours or more, be sure to reconfirm your onward flight with the airline during your stay. If you fail to do this, the airline can cancel your reservation even if you have a ticket in hand. Call the airline or have the hotel concierge or business centre handle this for you.

Airlines Serving Taiwan

China Airlines, Far Eastern Airlines, Formosa Airlines, Trans-Asia Airlines, Taiwan Airlines, Great China Airlines and Makung Airlines operate many daily flights between the main cities of Taipei and Kaohsiung. Several of the airlines also serve the smaller cities of Tainan, Taichung, Chiyi, Hualien and Taitung, as well as the offshore islands of Green Island, Lanyu (Orchid Island), Penghu and Kinmen.

Airport to Hotel Transportation

A cost efficient way to get to the city is by limousine bus. Buses leave every 15 to 20 minutes from the terminal. One-way tickets from CKS Airport to Taipei cost NT$115. The trip usually takes 60–90 minutes.

A taxi is much more expensive than the bus, but if you are weary from a long flight and have with you heavy luggage, it is worth the expense. Because taxis have to wait in long queues at the airport, a 50% surcharge is allowed over the fare shown on the taxi meter for trips from CKS Airport. The average fare (plus surcharge) to Taipei is about NT$1,000–$1,200. Make sure the meter is running when the car starts to move. If the meter is not working, decide on a price before the car moves.

Major hotels provide hotel limousines and shuttle buses to and from the airport for their guests, usually for a fee—a substantial fee for a private car.

If you are arriving in Taipei on a domestic flight from down-island, you will land at Taipei's Sungshan Airport in the middle of the city. Take a taxi from here to your destination.

Business Hours

Most business and government offices are open Monday through Friday from 8.30 a.m. to noon, and from 1.30 p.m. to 5.30 p.m. Most are also open on Saturdays from 8.30 a.m. to noon. Banks are open from 9 a.m. to 3.30 p.m., Monday through Friday, and 9 a.m. to noon on Saturdays.

Do not be surprised to see workers sleeping at their desks after lunch. Lunch hours are long for a reason—to allow time to relax and digest the food before diving back into work.

Twenty-four-hour shopping has arrived in Taiwan. Convenience store chains are often open round the clock, seven days a week. Other small shops open early in the morning and are closed on Sundays.

Climate and Clothing

Taipei can be cold (as low as 10°C) and damp in winter so bring along warm clothing. Northern Taiwan can be considerably colder

Taiwan's Temperature Guide

Months	Temperature (°C, min–max)	Humidity*	Attire
Jan–March	12–21	84	Medium to heavy
Apr–June	17–32	83	Light to medium
July–Sept	23–33	79	Light
Oct–Dec	14–27	81	Sweaters/jackets

than the south in winter. The mountains of central Taiwan can also be quite cold. However, in the far south, swimming is possible all year round.

For summer travel, bring lightweight cotton clothes, as the heat and humidity can make one rather miserable. In Taiwan's office towers, business suits and ties for men are the norm. Go without a tie or jacket only if your Taiwanese counterparts do so. It rains a lot in Taiwan, so keep an umbrella or raincoat handy.

Crime

In 1997, about 13,000 cases of murder, rape, robbery and other violent crimes were reported in Taiwan, double the figure a decade ago. Despite this rise, very little crime is directed against foreigners in the country. The cities are relatively safe for solitary pedestrians, even at night. Do not, however, take unnecessary risks. Walking down a dark alley draped in gold jewellery is unwise in any country, including Taiwan.

Currency

Taiwan's unit of currency is the New Taiwan dollar (NT$). Foreign currency can be exchanged at government-designated banks, hotels and airport exchange windows. Taiwan does not have private money-changers, unlike Hong Kong and parts of Southeast Asia, due to government prohibition. Receipts are given when currency is exchanged and these must be presented in order to exchange unused NT dollars before departure.

Major credit cards are accepted and traveller's cheques may be exchanged for money at most tourist shops, banks and airports and by room guests at international tourist hotels. Many banks charge a fee for each cheque cashed.

Customs

Passengers may not bring in or leave with more than NT$40,000 in cash without a permit from the Central Bank of China. You may not leave Taiwan with more than US$5,000 in cash or its equivalent in other currencies, unless declared upon arrival. Personal belongings are duty-free, but stereo equipment and video recorders must be declared.

Up to one litre of alcoholic beverages, 25 cigars, 200 cigarettes or one pound of tobacco are allowed into the country, duty free. Duty is charged on gold in excess of 62.5 grams.

Electricity

Taiwan has a reliable power generation system and blackouts are rare. The electric current is 110 volts, 60 cycles, AC, the same as in the United States and Canada. You will need transformers to operate appliances from Europe, Southeast Asia and Australia in Taiwan.

Geography

Shaped like a tobacco leaf, the island of Taiwan lies 160 km east of the Chinese mainland coastal province of Fujian. The island is 395 km north to south and 144 km in maximum width.

The island is just over 35,980 sq km in total area, a little larger than Canada's Vancouver Island. Taiwan's highest peak, Yushan (Jade Mountain), is 3,952 metres high—higher than Japan's Mount Fuji.

Taiwan's eastern coast is mountainous and not heavily populated. The precipitous cliffs overhanging the ocean from Hualien to Taitung are one of the most scenic areas in East Asia. Taiwan's western coast is a flat and fertile plain, sloping down to the Taiwan Straits from the central mountains. Most of the country's population lives on this plain that stretches from Taipei in the north to Kaohsiung in the south.

Tourists can visit the tiny Penghu Islands in the Taiwan Straits.

The ROC government also controls three islands off the coast of Fujian Province—Kinmen, Matsu and Wuchiu. These islands captured the world's attention in the early 1960s when they were heavily shelled by the PRC forces in a vain attempt to dislodge the Nationalists.

Health Matters

Taiwan's drinking water is generally safe, especially in the cities. There are trace chemicals in the municipal water supply, but this is not hazardous unless you drink it over a long period of time. Hotel tap water is not necessarily safe to drink, but the water provided in thermos bottles and served at the table is generally safe. It is safest to drink coffee or hot tea since the water used is boiled.

While the levels of residual pesticides left on fruit and vegetables have been declining, be careful when eating them raw. Wash fruit and vegetables thoroughly before eating them.

Vaccinations
People who have been in cholera-infected areas must be inoculated more than seven days but less than six months before arrival. Because the incidence of Hepatitis B is high in Taiwan, some health officials recommend vaccinations against it. People are also advised to have a polio immunisation as the disease has not been fully eradicated.

When eating out, stick to clean eateries that serve hot, well-cooked dishes. It is risky to eat uncooked seafood, especially shellfish. Street stalls offers a unique eating experience, but before eating at any of them, check out the dishwashing method. If dishes are washed in dirty, soapy buckets of water, stay clear!

Monosodium Glutamate or MSG is a flavour enhancer that is commonly used in Chinese cooking but can cause adverse reactions in some people, especially asthma sufferers. Side effects can include nausea, abdominal pain and headaches. Soups usually contain higher concentrations of MSG.

Do not use the hot or cold towels provided in restaurants or on trains near the eyes. Conjunctivitis is a common problem.

Holidays

Public Hoidays in Taiwan

Holiday	Gregorian Calendar
New Year's Day	1–2 January
Chinese New Year	Late January/February (1st day of the 1st moon)
Youth Day	29 March
Women's and Children's Day	3 April
Tomb Sweeping Day	April
Dragon Boat Festival	June (5th day of 5th lunar month)
Mid-Autumn Festival	September (15th day of the 8th lunar month)
Confucius' Birthday (Teacher's Day)	28 September
Double Tenth Day	10 October
Taiwan Retrocession Day	25 October
Chiang Kai-shek's Birthday	31 October
Sun Yat-sen's Birthday	12 November
Constitution Day	25 December

Some of Taiwan's holidays are set according to the Gregorian calendar while other more traditional holidays are set according to the Lunar calendar.

In order to introduce a long weekend, the authorities may announce a shifting of the working half-day on Saturdays. For instance, if Teacher's Day (28 September) occurs on a Friday, the next day (29 September, Saturday) will be declared a holiday. However, people have to work all-day the next Saturday (6 October) to make up for it.

Hotels
Taiwan's business hotels range from luxury international tourist hotels to budget "business hotels". Most major hotels in Taipei are located on and around Chungshan North Road or in the eastern part of the city near the Taipei World Trade Centre. The room rates in Taipei's top hotels are rather high. Accommodation in the other cities are more reasonably priced.

For a weekend retreat, try the hot springs resorts scattered all over the island. Some offer Japanese-style inns, complete with sliding screen doors and *tatami* mats for sleeping.

Hotel Business Centres
Stay in hotels with business service centres. In the better hotels, the staff usually speak English and can help you with many chores, from getting your business cards translated into Chinese to sending faxes. Most also have a business library that includes Taiwan business directories and other reference books that can be used for business research or meeting preparations.

Hotel Business Centres Services
The following are standard charges for services offered by most of Taipei's hotel business centres:

Secretarial Services	NT$500/hour
Typing	NT$300/page
Photocopying	NT$10/page
Laser Print-outs	NT$50/page
Incoming fax	Complimentary
Outgoing fax	Local: NT$50/page
	Asia: NT$180/page
	USA/Canada/Australia: NT$200/page
	Europe and others: NT$200/page
Translation/Interpretation	Cost + 20% service charge
Business card printing	Cost + 20% service charge
Courier Service	Cost + 20% service charge

Equipment Rental	Rental/day	Deposit
Portable fax machine	NT$250	–
Portable electric typewriter	NT$200	NT$5,000
Dictaphone	NT$200	NT$5,000
Pager	NT$200	NT$3,000
Overhead Projector	NT$1,500	–
Internet use	NT$10/minute	–

Pharmaceuticals
Most over-the-counter medicines and brand-name cosmetics are available in hotel arcades, chain stores and drugstores.

Radio
The main English-language radio station, International Community Radio Taipei (ICRT), broadcasts on FM100.7 Mhz and AM576 Khz. BBC and Radio France are frequently relayed over ICRT at AM576 Khz.

If you want to keel abreast of the latest happenings in Taiwan via shortwave radio, listen to "The Voice of Free China" in English on 5950, 7130, 9680, 9850, 9955, 11740, 11745, 11825, 15215, and 17845 KHz. To get an updated transmission schedule, write to "The Voice of Free China", P.O. Box 24–38, Taipei, Taiwan ROC.

Religion

Most Taiwanese are Buddhists. Buddhist temples, shrines and statues are found all over the country. The oldest and best-known Buddhist temple in Taipei is Lungshan Temple, which is about 250 years old. In Mandarin, *lungshan* means "dragon hill"; the temple is always filled with worshippers. The Chinese and Taiwanese do not usually go to group services. They go to the temple individually when they have a desire to do so.

In addition to Buddhism, Confucianism and Taoism are also important philosophies in Taiwan. The Taiwanese are tolerant of religion and many people have no qualms about considering themselves to be simultaneously Buddhist, Confucian, Taoist and even Christian.

Shopping

Bargaining is still common in Taiwan, especially in street markets and family-owned retail shops. Most up-market retail stores have fixed prices. Most jewellery shops invite bargaining. Begin by offering half the asking price and proceed from there. The more naive (i.e. foreign) you appear, the higher will be the quoted price. Many shops will insist on tacking on about 4% extra if you use a credit card for your purchase.

Taiwanese pink coral jewellery is often a good bargain; along with granite carvings from Hualien, it is one of the few Taiwanese indigenous handicraft readily available to tourists. Curio and jewellery shops abound in the country. If you are in the Taipei World Trade Centre, you will find a wide variety of jewellery in the shops at the exhibition centre.

Some of the most interesting souvenirs available are the handicraft found in the Buddhist shops near Lungshan (Dragon

Mountain) Temple in the old section of Taipei and other temples on the island. Everything that one cannot find in a 7-11 can be found here—fortune-telling bamboo rulers, porcelain deities, bronze gongs, red candles, brass incense urns and even evil-looking sticks studded with sharks teeth for those who want to punish the "demons" within themselves. My favourite is the carved image of rosy-cheeked Wen Chang, the god of literature. He is popular with high-school students trying to pass college entrance exams.

Taiwan Stock Exchange
For up-to-date information about the Taiwan Stock Exchange, look up its web page on the Internet. This web page shows the trade value, transactions, open price, highest price, lowest price and closing price, together with the capitalisation weighted stock index, for the market closing.

Telegraph/Telex/Fax
Most hotels have business centres that provide these services. Telegram facilities are available at the main ITA office.

Telephones
Public pay phones are plentiful and easy to find. Local calls cost NT$1 for every three minutes. Long-distance calls can also be made from public pay phones. Green phones take NT$1, NT$5 and NT$10 coins. Overseas calls can be made direct to most countries from major hotels or international public card phones by dialling the code 002 followed by the destination code. The fee for international direct dialling is calculated every six seconds. NT$100 stored-value cards for beige card-phones can be used for long distance calls and are available at convenience stores and hotel shops.

On private phones, the overseas operator may be reached by dialling "100". Direct dialling is also available. Person-to-person

A Word of Caution
To avoid hotel surcharges and the high charges of Taiwan's telephone system, use payphones in hotel lobbies and utilise calling card plans offered by phone companies in your home country, such as USA Direct and Korea Direct. Such services bill you based on your home country's telephone rates—often less expensive than the rates charged by Taiwan's telecommunications systems. Check with your long-distance service company about this service before leaving home.

and station-to-station calls are accepted. Call the International Telecommunications Administration (ITA), Ministry of Transportation and Communication, for further information.

To obtain phone numbers in Taiwan, contact the Directory Assistance (English-speaking) provided by the ITA.

All the telephone numbers in the Taipei and Keelung areas were converted from seven to eight digits on 1 January 1998.

Time
Taiwan is eight hours ahead of Greenwich Mean Time (GMT) with no daylight savings adjustment. Taiwan shares its time zone with mainland China, Singapore, Malaysia, the Philippines, central Indonesia and Western Australia.

Tipping
A 10% service charge (plus 5% VAT) is usually added to bills in hotels and good restaurants. The suggested tip in hotels is NT$50 per piece of luggage. All other tipping is optional.

Visas
All visitors to Taiwan are required to have valid entry visas through the embassies or consulates of the ROC or from an authorised overseas representative office. There is visa-free entry for nationals

of 20 countries entering Taiwan for 14 days or less. The visa-free service, first introduced in January 1995, is applicable to Australia, Austria, Belgium, Canada, France, Germany, Japan, Luxembourg, the Netherlands, New Zealand, Portugal, Spain, Sweden, the United Kingdom, the United States, Switzerland, Italy, Poland, the Czech Republic and Hungary. The requirements for the 14-day visa-free entry are:

- Valid passports for at least six months
- Onward airline (steamship) ticket confirmed within 14 days
- No violation of law recorded

Landing Visa

Citizens of the above 20 countries may apply for a 30-day landing visa upon arrival for transit to another destination on the condition that they:

- Hold a valid passport with validity of more than six months
- Possess a confirmed airline ticket that indicates that the holder is to leave Taiwan within 30 days
- Pay the visa fee of NT$1,500
- Submit one identification photo

If it is necessary to stay more than 14 days but less than 30 days, the nationals of the specified countries should apply for landing visas with the visa office in the Chiang Kai-shek Airport from MOEA near the immigration gates. The landing visa fee is NT$1,500.

Visitor Visas

Two-week to 60-day visitor visas are granted to foreign nationals who visit Taiwan for tourism, study, training, business, to see relatives and other legitimate reasons.

Those who hold visitor visas valid for 60 days may apply for extension. No extension will be granted to those holding visitor visas with a validity of less than 60 days, except for situations caused by *force majeure*, or "matters of vital importance".

Application Fees

Foreign nationals from countries with reciprocal visa agreements with Taiwan can usually obtain visitor visas without a charge. For other foreign nationals, visitor visa fees are NT$1,000 for a single entry and NT$2,000 for multiple entry visas.

If you are going to travel to Taiwan for the purpose of business, you do not need the sponsorship of a Taiwan company or agency.

Visa regulations and policies change arbitrarily, so always check with the visa section of ROC embassies/consulates or authorised representatives to make certain you are meeting the latest requirements for obtaining visas.

Water

Boiled or distilled water is recommended. Drinking water served at hotels and restaurants is normally distilled or boiled. Avoid tap water outside the hotels. Bottled mineral water is widely available in hotels and convenience stores.

What to Bring

In addition to business attire, other things to bring include:

- A collapsible umbrella that can fit into a briefcase
- Gift-wrapping paper for business gifts
- Gifts or mementos as presentation
- Electric outlet converters and voltage regulator for laptop computers
- Several extra copies of passport-sized photographs. Keep a photocopy of your passport and visa separate from the originals. If you lose the originals, copies will help expedite their replacement.

Directory of Important Contacts

Republic of China on Taiwan Government Agencies and Ministries

Bureau of Commodity Inspection and Quarantine
4 Chi Nan Rd., Sec. 1
Taipei
Tel: 343-1700
Fax: 393-2324

China External Trade Development Council (CETRA)
International Trade Building, 4-7F
#333 Keelung Rd., Sec 1
Taipei
Tel: 725-5200
Fax: 757-6653

Directorate General of Customs
85 Hsin Sheng S. Rd., Sec. 1
Taipei
Tel: 550-5522

Environmental Protection Administration
41 Chung Hwa Rd., Sec. 1
Taipei
Tel: 311-7722
Fax: 311-6071

Ministry of Finance
2 Ai Kuo W. Rd.
Taipei
Tel: 322-8000
Fax: 321-1205

Ministry of Foreign Affairs
2 Kai Ta Ke Lan Blvd
Taipei
Tel: 311-9292

Government Information Office
2 Tien Tsin St.
Taipei
Tel: 322-8888
Fax: 356-8733

Bureau of Health
1 Shih Fu Rd.
Taipei
Tel: 720-8898
Fax: 759-3002

Bureau of Labour Affairs
1 Shih Fu Rd
Taipei
Tel: 720-8898
Fax: 720-9339

Ministry of Transportation and Communication, Tourism Bureau
9F, #280 Chung Hsiao E. Rd., Sec 4
Taipei
Tel: 349-1500
Fax: 773-5487

Ministry of Transportation and Communication
2 Chang Sha St., Sec 1
Taipei
Tel: 349-2900
Fax: 389-6009

Industrial Development Bureau
41-3 Hsinyi Rd., Sec. 3, Taipei
Tel: 886-22-7541255
Fax: 886-22-7030160

Board of Foreign Trade
1 Hukou St., Taipei
Tel: 886-22-3510271
Fax: 886-22-3513603

National Bureau of Standards
3F, 185 Hsinhai Rd., Sec. 2, Taipei
Tel: 886-22-7380007
Fax: 886-22-7352656

Ministry of Economic Affairs (MOEA)

Bureau of Commodity Inspection & Quarantine
4 Chinan Rd., Sec. 1, Taipei
Tel: 886-22-3431700
Fax: 886-22-3560998

Water Resources Planning
10F, 41-3 Hsinyi Rd., Sec. 3, Taipei
Tel: 886-22-7542080
Fax: 886-22-7542244

Small & Medium Business
Administration
3F, 95 Roosevelt Rd., Sec. 2, Taipei
Tel: 886-22-3680816
Fax: 886-22-3673883

Export Processing Zone
Administration
600 Chiachang Rd.,
Nantze, Kaohsiung
Tel: 886-7-3611212
Fax: 886-7-3614348

Central Geological Survey
2, Lane 109, Huahsin St., Chungho,
Taipei hsien
Tel: 886-22-9462793
Fax: 886-22-9429291

Investment Commission
8F, Yumin Bldg., 7 Roosevelt Rd., Sec.
1, Taipei
Tel: 886-22-23513151
Fax: 886-22-3964207

Energy Commission
12F, 2 Fuhsing N. Rd., Taipei
Tel: 886-22-7721370
Fax: 886-22-7769417

Commission of National
Corporations
25 Paoching Rd., Taipei
Tel: 886-22-3713161
Fax: 886-22-3825554

Trade Investigation Commission
5 Hsinyi Rd., Sec 5, Taipei
Tel: 886-22-7589566
Fax: 886-22-7232281

Professional Training Centre
3 Kuangfu Rd., Sec. 2, Hsinchu
Tel: 886-35-716124
Fax: 886-35-722364

International Economic
Cooperation Development Fund
7F, No.51 Sec.7 Chung-Ching S. Rd.,
Taipei, Taiwan. R.O.C.

Taiwan's Major Industrial Associations

Taiwan Electrical & Electronic
Manufacturers Association
Fl. 10, No. 10, Lane 609, Chung-
Hsin Road, Sec. 5, San-Chung City,
Taipei
Tel: 02-999-2828
Fax: 02-999-2626

Taiwan Plastics Industry
Association
Fl. 8, No. 162, Sec. 2, Ch'ang-An E.
Road, Taipei
Tel: 02-7719111
Fax: 02-7315020

Taiwan Association of Machinery
Industry
Fl. 2, No. 110, Huai-Ning Street,
Taipei
Tel: 02-3813722
Fax: 02-3813711

Petrochemical Industry Association
of Taiwan
 Fl. 9-2, No. 390, Sec. 1, Fu-Hsing
S. Road, Taipei
Tel: 02-7073018
Fax: 02-7555154

Taiwan Medical Industrial
Association
Fl. 8, No. 201-18, Tun-Hwa N.
Road, Taipei
Tel: 02-7123063
Fax: 02-7123071

Taiwan Steel Wire & Wire Rope
Industries Association
Fl. 5, No. 369, Fu-Hsing N. Road,
Taipei
Tel: 02-7155032
Fax: 02-7182546

Taiwan Regional Engineering
Contractors Association
Fl. 10, No.21, Sec. 1, Chan-An E.
Road, Taipei
Tel: 02-5810188
Fax: 02-5180091

Taiwan Cosmetics & Toiletries
Industry Association
Fl. 5, No. 136, Po-Ai Road, Taipei
Tel: 02-3819700
Fax: 02-3611584

Taiwan Agricultural Machinery
Manufacturers Association
Ground Fl., No. 273, Kwen-Ming
Street, Taipei
Tel: 02-3365718
Fax: 02-3365719

Taiwan Electric Power Association
Fl. 11, No. 242, Sec. 3, Rosevelt
Road, Taipei
Tel: 02-3667328
Fax: 02-3656869

Taiwan Frozen Food Processors
Association
Rm. 2, Fl. 11, No. 103, Chung-
Cheng 4th Road, Kaohsiung
Tel: 07-2412053
Fax: 07-2412055

Banks

The Central Bank of China
2 Roosevelt Road
Sec 1, Taipei
Tel: (2) 393-6161
Fax: (2) 397-3750

Chang Hwa Commercial
Bank Ltd.
57 Chung Shan N. Rd
Sec 2, Taipei
Tel: (2) 536-2951

Hua Nan Commercial Bank Ltd.
38 Chungking S. Rd
Sec 1, Taipei
Tel: (2) 371-3111
Fax: (2) 331-5737

Overseas Chinese Commercial
Banking Corporation
8 Hsiang Yang Rd
Taipei
Tel: (2) 371-5181
Fax: (2) 381-4056

Shanghai Commercial & Savings
Bank Ltd.
16 Jen Ai Rd
Sec 2, Taipei
Tel: (2) 393-3111
Fax: (2) 392-8391

Taipei Bank
50 Chung Shan N. Rd
Sec 2, Taipei
Tel: (2) 542-5656
Fax: (2) 523-1235

United World Chinese
Commercial Bank
65 Kuan Chien Rd
Taipei
Tel: (2) 312-5555
Fax: (2) 331-8263

Business and Market Consultants

Deloitte & Touche
102 Kuang S. Rd
Taipei
Tel: (2) 741-0258
Fax: (2) 776-321

Diwan, Ernst & Young
9F, #333 Keelung Rd
Sec 1, Taipei
Tel: 720-4000
Fax: 757-6050

Field Force Integrated Marketing
13F, 137 Nanking E. Rd
Sec 2, Taipei
Tel: (2) 515-6288

Frank Small & Associates
3F, 34 Pateh Rd
Sec 3, Taipei
Tel: (2) 577-5505
Fax: (2) 577-4807

Dun & Bradstreet International Ltd
12/F, 188 Nanking E. Rd
Sec 5, Taipei
Tel: (2) 756-2922
Fax: (2) 749-1936

McKinsey & Company Inc.
Suite A, 19F,
167 Tun Hwa N. Rd
Taipei
Tel: (2) 718-2223

T.N. Soong & Co.
12F, Hung Tai Century Tower
156 Min Sheng E. Rd
Sec 3, Taipei
Tel: (2) 545-9988

Law firms

Baker & McKenzie
15F, #168 Tun Hua N. Rd.
Taipei
Tel: 712-6151
Fax: 716-9250

**Broughton, Peterson,
Yang & Anderson**
2F #303 Tun Hua N. Rd
Taipei
Tel: 713-8681
Fax: 719-2145

Century International
8F-6, #50 Hsin Sheng S. Rd., Sec 1
Taipei
Tel: 395-6858
Fax: 341-0370

Chen, Chang & Associates
3F-7, #2 Fu Hsing N. Rd.
Taipei
Tel: 741-5091
Fax: 741-5090

Cheng & Cheng Law Office
17F, #123 Chung Hsiao E. Rd., Sec 2
Taipei
Tel: 713-3233
Fax: 713-3222

Lee & Li
7F, #201 Tun Hua N. Rd.
Taipei
Tel: 715-3300
Fax: 713-3966

Concordia Consulting Ltd.
Suite 704, #432 Keelung Rd., Sec 1
Taipei
Tel: 729-8976
Fax: 729-0268

Perkins Coie
8F, #85 Jen Ai Rd., Sec 4
Taipei
Tel: 778-1177
Fax: 777-9808

Deacons Graham and Jones
7F, #54 Chung Shan N. Rd. Sec 3
Taipei
Tel: 597-4521
Fax: 592-6601

Russin & Vecchi
9F, Rm 901, #205 Tun Hua N. Rd.
Taipei
Tel: 713-6110
Fax: 713-4711

Translation Services

President Translation Service
11F-6, #1 Fu Hsing N. Rd.
Taipei
Tel: 731-2483
Fax: 752-6464

Taipei Translation Centre
4F-1, #206 Sung Chiang Rd
Taipei
Tel: 542-8558
Fax: 543-2979

Pristine Communications
10F, #171 Roosevelt Rd., Sec 3
Taipei
Tel: 368-9023
Fax: 367-0342

Chambers of Commerce

American Chamber of Commerce
Rm. 1012, 96 Chung Shan N.
Road, Section 2, Taipei
Tel: (02) 581 7089
Fax: (02) 567 5726

British Chamber of Commerce
7F, 99 Jen Ai Road,
Section 2, Taipei
Tel: (02) 356 0210
Fax: (02) 356 0211

Canadian Trade Office in Taipei
365 Fu Hsing North Road, 13th
Floor Taipei, 10483, Taiwan
Tel: (011-886-2) 547-9500
Fax: (011-886-2) 712-7244

**Chinese National Assn. of
Industry & Commerce**
13F, 390 Fu Hsing S. Road,
Section 1, Taipei
Tel: (02) 703 3500
Fax: (02) 703 3982

**Confederation of Asia Pacific
Chamber of Commerce & Industry**
10F, 122 Tun Hua N. Road,
Section 1, Taipei
Tel: (02) 716 3016
Fax: (02) 718 3683

**French Chamber of Commerce &
Industry**
Rm. 7B01, 5 Hsin Yi Road,
Section5, Taipei
Tel: (02) 723 2740
Fax: (02) 723 2743

**General Chamber of Commerce
of the ROC**
6F, 390 Fu Hsing S. Road,
Section 1, Taipei
Tel: (02) 701 2671
Fax: (02) 754 2107

Indonesian Chamber of Commerce
3F, 46-1 Chung Cheng Road,
Section2, Taipei
Tel: (02) 831 0451
Fax: (02) 836 1844

Kaohsiung Chamber of Commerce
8 Chien Kuang Road, Kaohsiung
Tel: (07) 531 8121
Fax: (02) 521 7761

Spanish Chamber of Commerce
7F-1, 602 Tun Hua S. Road,
Taipei
Tel: (02) 325 6234
Fax: (02) 754 2572

Taipei Chamber of Commerce
6F, 72 Nan King E. Road,
Section 2, Taipei
Tel: (02) 531 8217
Fax: (02) 542 9461

Taiwan Chamber of Commerce
4F, 158 Sung Chiang Road,
Taipei
Tel: (02) 536 5455
Fax: (02) 521 1980

Understanding Taiwan through the Internet

The business person determined to understand Taiwan and its people can turn to the Internet for both research and news. One of the best sources of information can be found in the Usenet newsgroups about Taiwan. The Usenet newsgroup, "soc.culture.taiwan" (SCT), discusses about all things Taiwanese is one of the most useful. This newsgroup can be found at: http://www.geocities.com/~tyang/Taiwan_faq.html

On "soc.culture.taiwan", participants discuss Taiwanese culture, including its customs, food, language, politics and related topics. For historical reasons, a lot of messages about things Chinese and Taiwanese are crossposted in "soc.culture.china" and "soc.culture.taiwan".

You should also check out another Usenet newsgroup called "alt.taiwan.republic", which, while less active than SCT, contains information not posted on SCT.

If you have access to Chinese character software, you can also try the newsgroup "alt.chinese.text.big5", in which participants post their ideas in Chinese characters

Remember when posting your questions or ideas on the newsgroups that commercial advertising is not welcome. Violators will be flamed, the Internet equivalent of being stoned as a sinner. You will be on the receiving end of many caustic e-mail protestations. Users of the newsgroups are interested in two-way discussions about things Taiwanese and not the wonderful products you have to sell. Before using the newsgroups, be sure to read their rules.

The following answers to frequently asked questions (FAQs) about Taiwan were adapted with permission from the Internet-based *"soc.culture.taiwan" Survival Guide and Frequently Asked Questions* by Tung-chiang Yang (tcyang@netcom.com).

Frequently Asked Questions

Is there any on-line map for Taiwan?
Yes. Try the home web page at:
http://www.lib.utexas.edu/Libs/PCL/Map_collection/Map_collection.html

Click at the entry "Maps of Asia" and then the entry "Taiwan (283K)". This CIA-prepared map includes the names of major cities, a rough topology, rivers, railroads, freeways and county boundaries. It may be the most detailed map of Taiwan currently available on the Internet.

You can find another on-line map at: http://peacock.tnjc.edu.tw/ADD/maps/taiwanmap.html, which provides an interactive mechanism so you can zoom into details of different parts of Taiwan, although information about the central mountainous area may be limited.

Geosystems Global Corp. provides an on-line street map for Taipei at: http://www.mapquest.com/, where you can dig out the street map for Taipei with zooming capability, although not all streets are shown in detail for this map.

Where can I get on-line information about Taiwan's stock market?
You can try Taiwan Stock Exchange's web page at: http://www.tse.com.tw/mi/mi_stockE.html

This page shows the trade volume, trade value, transactions, open price, highest price, lowest price and close price, together with the capitalization weighted stock index, for the market closing. The URL for this page often changes. If what you see above becomes obsolete, start with: http://www.tse.com.tw/.

For some companies in the list, general information like address and phone numbers and financial information like turnover, operating profit and earnings per share are also available for the previous three years.

Where can I get information about teaching English in Taiwan?
You can try the web page at: http://www.u-net.com/eflweb/taiwan0.html

The author, Hall Houston, spent a few years in Taipei and taught English there. You can ask him some questions not covered in the above web page (or if you do not have access to the World Wide Web, or WWW) by sending e-mails to him at "hhouston@mail.utexas.edu".

Is there any on-line information about libraries in Taiwan?
You can try to telnet the following IP addresses: "opac.ncl.edu.tw" (National Central Library. Login and password: "ncl") and "pyd.ksml.edu.tw" (Kaohsiung Municipal Library; login: "library"). However, to make full use of these facilities, you need to have a Chinese system installed.

Is there any on-line "newspaper" in Taiwan?
Yes. You can read Taiwan Headline News provided by Central News Agency at the URL of SinaNet: http://ww3.sinanet.com/news/index_taiwan.html and http://ww3.sinanet.com/news/MMDDnews/index_C.html

The former refers to the news today. In the latter URL, you can change "MMDD" to choose to read a specific day's news. For instance, replace "MMDD" with 0624 to read the news from 24 June. The advantage of this site is that all Chinese text are represented by "gif" file format, so you can read news in Chinese even if your web browser cannot decode Big-5, or Chinese text in html format. Big-5, a Chinese language computing environment, supports up to 13,000 Chinese characters and is really only suitable for basic communication purposes. Most Chinese dictionaries, by contrast, include 56,000 characters.

Quintet Inc. also provides a similar on-line news service at: http://w3.ttnn.com/cna/index.html for which you do not need a Chinese environment to read Chinese news. This site also keeps the news articles archived and available for months.

China Times has also set up its homepage. The URL is at: http://www.chinatimes.com.tw/ and http://chinatimes.nsysu.edu.tw/, both of which work equally well. You can also try the US mirror site at: http://www.chinatimes.com/.

If you want to read "real-time" news, you can go directly to the URL at: http://www.tol.com.tw/rtnews/html/rtnews.html.

Ming-shen Daily News, in collaboration with the Department of Education, Taiwan Provincial Government, has set up its WWW at: http://msdn.aide.gov.tw/.

Commercial Times has its WWW with Taiwan-on-Line at: http://www.tol.com.tw/READING/HTML/reading.htm, which is also related to *China Times*.

New Asian Weekly also provides its WWW site in cyberspace. You can first go to http://www.newasian.com/naw.htm and then to the NAW site. Nevertheless, a Big-5 environment is needed.

Liberty Times set up its WWW site at: http://libertytimes.nsysu.edu.tw/, while its US edition, *Chinese Los Angeles Daily News*, is at: http://www.chinesedaily.com/. Both GIF and Big-5 are provided.

China Economic News Service claims to be the largest business news service provider in Taiwan. You can visit their WWW site at: http://www.cens.com/.

For the political magazine, *The Journalist* (New News), you can try http://journalist.cybereye.net.tw/. You will need Big-5 environment to read most of the materials on this site.

Is there any on-line information about jobs in Taiwan?

Yes. For gopher, you can use "gopher.nyc.gov.tw" to browse through information about job conditions and starting a new business in Taiwan. Chinese environments are required for this database provided by the National Youth Commission under the executive yuan. You can also use telnet to access the information.

The following web sites provide links to job-related ads in Taiwan. Individuals can leave their resumes there and companies can also post their requirements for potential employees. Some fees may be accessed. These sites can be found at: http://www.job.com.tw/ and http://www.104.com.tw/.

Is there any World Wide Web page for Taiwan?

Yes, there are some. If you have a WWW browser, you can start at the home web page of Jon A. Nunez made at: http://peacock.tnjc.edu.tw/ROC.HTML. This page briefly explains the political structure of the Republic of China.

You can also try http://peacock.tnjc.edu.tw/ROC_sites.html, which is jointly maintained by the Computer Centre or Ministry of Education, ROC, Tung Nan Junior College of Technology, Yimin Hu at "yimin@moers2.edu.tw" and Joe Hsu at "joe@peacock.tnjc.edu.tw". This page provides information about Taiwan and the ROC, and some technical information about miscellaneous networks in Taiwan, like some Bulletin Board Systems (BBS) that computer users with modems can dial up to without going through the Internet. The selection "General Information" includes a lot of useful data about Taiwan. Some Chinese environment (like Big-5) will be helpful.

The WWW site, "peacock.tnjc.edu.tw", was the first one established in Taiwan.

The Government Information Office has a WWW page at: http://www.gio.gov.tw, which can be viewed as an official web page for the ROC government on Taiwan. This page is available in French, Spanish, German, Japanese and Chinese. The 1996 yearbook provides a detailed description about Taiwan and many statistics are also available. The yearbook is located at: http://www.gio.gov.tw:80/info/yearbook/index.html.

The WWW site of the Directorate General of Budget, Accounting and Statistics of the executive yuan provides some official statistics of Taiwan, like population, marital status of individuals, mass media services, government of the Republic of China, and so on. You can go to http://www.dgbasey.gov.tw/english/english.htm for more information.

If you are interested in knowing Taiwan from an American viewpoint, try the WWW page of the Central Intelligence Agency (CIA), U.S.A. at http://www.odci.gov/cia and then choose "Taiwan" under the entries "CIA Publications", "The World Factbook 1996" and "Asia", or use http://www.odci.gov/cia/publications/nsolo/factbook/tw.htm.

The Taiwanese Student Association of the University of Texas at Austin, U.S.A., also worked on a good web page for Taiwan. You can view it at http://www.utexas.edu:80/ftp/student/tsa/.

Miscellaneous universities, institutions and high schools have also created their own web pages. The corresponding URL address can be formed by replacing the "xxx" in http://www.xxx.[edu,gov,org].tw., with the Internet host address reserved for that school, which can be found in the "Internet Addresses in Taiwan" section below.

The web page at http://www.roc.com/impexp/ provides a search base for 14,000 leading firms and 5,000 select commodities in Taiwan for import and export purposes. The data is from the Customs Bureau. This may be useful for business-oriented people. On the other hand, the URL at http://www.roc.com/assn/ provides a list of official trade associations in Taiwan.

YamWeb Navigator may be considered the "Yahoo" in Taiwan. It provides a search engine in Chinese (Big5). You can reach it at http://taiwan.csie.ntu.edu.tw/bin/yam, where you can start your navigation.

Li & Partners set up a legal data bank for laws in Taiwan and mainland China. It includes both the constitutions of the Republic of China and the People's Republic of China, and some related items like the Republic of China constitution amendments and the basic laws for the Hongkong Special District. You can reach it at http://www.law.com.tw/ and begin your legal experience.

Internet Addresses in Taiwan

The top-level domain name for most Internet addresses in Taiwan is "tw". After stripping off the "tw", the remaining part of the addresses use the conventional notations, like "com" for commercial organizations, "edu" for educational organizations, "gov" for government agencies, "net" for networking organisations and "org" for non-profit organisations.

For Internet addresses that will take you directly to their homepage web sites, try:

- http://www.geocities.com/~tyang/sct_yellowpage1.html
- http://www.geocities.com/~tyang/sct_yellowpage2.html
- http://www.geocities.com/~tyang/sct_yellowpage3.html

Sources of Information

Books

American Chamber of Commerce in Taipei. *China Business Directory.* A guide to over 400 service/consulting firms with branches in Taiwan and China. Includes addresses, telephone and fax numbers, and contact names. Directory includes computer diskette version. Useful for job searches or entrepreneurs who need help setting up operations.

American Chamber of Commerce in Taipei. *A Guide to Doing Business in Taiwan*. Taipei, 1997.
An excellent and comprehensive guide to business in Taiwan. Includes valuable information about relevant procedures for setting up business operations.

American Chamber of Commerce in Taipei. *Taiwan Cost of Living Survey*. Taipei, 1996.
A reliable price index for living in Taipei, including supplemental information on housing, food, transportation, education, clothing, healthcare and entertainment. Essential for those considering a transfer to Taiwan.

CETRA. *Importers and Exporters in Taiwan, R.O.C.* Taipei, 1998.
Annually compiled directory of Taiwan's approximate 19,000 importers and exporters. Also available on CD-Rom.

CETRA. *Doing Business with Taiwan, R.O.C.*
Provides an overview on trade and business in Taiwan. A general information section gives practical hints for first-time visitors to the country.

Community Services Centre. *Taipei Living.* Taipei, 1997.
An excellent resource guide for expatriates living in Taipei.
Updated every two years.

Newsletters and Periodicals
American Chamber of Commerce in Taipei. *Topics* magazine.
Topics is the AmCham's in-house monthly, filled with articles
ranging from commercial and political issues to entertainment and
living in Taiwan.

Information about Taiwan on the Internet
American Chamber of Commerce in Taipei
http://www.amcham.com.tw

ABC – Taiwan Travel/Leisure
http://asiabiz.com/taiwan/travel/hotels.html
Guide to hotels in Taiwan

American Institute in Taiwan (AIT)
http://www.ait.org.tw

American Resource Center
http://www.arc.org.tw

China External Trade Association (CETRA)
http://www.tptaiwan.org.tw

Travel in Taiwan
http://www.sinica.edu.tw/tit/index.html

Asia, Inc. Online
http://www.asia-inc.com/index.html

Far East Economic Review
http://www.feer.com

Republic of China Yearbook
http://www.gio.gove\.tw/info/yearbook/index.html

Taiwan Stock Exchange
http://www.tse.com.tw

Taiwan Online / Taiwan Yellow Pages
http://www.twn-online.com.tw/english.html
Links to trade opportunities.

Taipei Economic & Cultural Office
http://www.taipei.org

SinaNet
http://www.sinanet.com
Includes a job resource center.

Trade Point
http://www.tradepoint.anjes.com.tw
Information on trade shows and a directory of companies.

In Asia
http://www.inasia.com
A large corporation database.

Trade Asia
http://www.TradeAsia.com
Telephone directory and database.

About the Author

KEVIN CHAMBERS is the director of the International Division of the State of Oklahoma Department of Commerce in the United States. He has worked as a Chinese translator for the US Army, as a US National Park Service ranger, as a university lecturer at Taiwan's Tunghai University, and as an international sales manager for a major US cable television company. He holds a masters degree in International Management from the American Graduate School of International Management (Thunderbird) and a BSc degree from Oklahoma State University.

The author of several books, including *Succeed in Business: Vietnam*, *The Travellers Guide to Asian Customs and Manners* and *The Travellers Guide to Asian Culture and History*, Kevin Chambers has lived and worked in South Korea and Taiwan. Since 1989, he has been helping American corporations to do business with Taiwan. He also conducts Taiwan-related business workshops. Kevin Chambers lives with his family in Tulsa, Oklahoma, USA.

Index